REGENTS RESTORATION DRAMA SERIES

General Editor: John Loftis

FATAL CURIOSITY

GEORGE LILLO

Fatal Curiosity

Edited by

William H. McBurney

UNIVERSITY OF NEBRASKA PRESS · LINCOLN

Library of Congress Catalog Card Number: 66–15130

MANUFACTURED IN THE UNITED STATES OF AMERICA

Regents Restoration Drama Series

The Regents Restoration Drama Series, similar in objectives and format to the Regents Renaissance Drama Series, will provide soundly edited texts, in modern spelling, of the more significant English plays of the late seventeenth and early eighteenth centuries. The word "Restoration" is here used ambiguously and must be explained. If to the historian it refers to the period between 1660 and 1685 (or 1688), it has long been used by the student of drama in default of a more precise word to refer to plays belonging to the dramatic tradition established in the 1660's, weakening after 1700, and displaced in the 1730's. It is in this extended sense—imprecise though justified by academic custom—that the word is used in this series, which will include plays first produced between 1660 and 1737. Although these limiting dates are determined by political events, the return of Charles II (and the removal of prohibitions against the operation of theaters) and the passage of Walpole's Stage Licensing Act, they enclose a period of dramatic history having a coherence of its own in the establishment, development, and disintegration of a tradition.

Each text in the series is based on a fresh collation of the seventeenth- and eighteenth-century editions that might be presumed to have authority. The textual notes, which appear above the rule at the bottom of each page, record all substantive departures from the edition used as the copy-text. Variant substantive readings among contemporary editions are listed there as well. Editions later than the eighteenth century are referred to in the textual notes only when an emendation originating in some one of them is received into the text. Variants of accidentals (spelling, punctuation, capitalization) are not recorded in the notes. Contracted forms of characters' names are silently expanded in speech prefixes and stage directions, and, in the case of speech prefixes, are regularized. Additions to the stage directions of the copy-text are enclosed in brackets. Stage directions such as "within" or "aside" are enclosed in parentheses when they occur in the copy-text.

Spelling has been modernized along consciously conservative lines, but within the limits of a modernized text the linguistic quality of the original has been carefully preserved. Contracted preterites have regularly been expanded. Punctuation has been brought into accord with modern practices. The objective has been to achieve a balance between the pointing of the old editions and a system of punctuation which, without overloading the text with exclamation marks, semicolons, and dashes, will make the often loosely flowing verse and prose of the original syntactically intelligible to the modern reader. Dashes are regularly used only to indicate interrupted speeches, or shifts of address within a single speech.

Explanatory notes, chiefly concerned with glossing obsolete words and phrases, are printed below the textual notes at the bottom of each page. References to stage directions in the notes follow the admirable system of the Revels editions, whereby stage directions are keyed, decimally, to the line of the text before or after which they occur. Thus, a note on 0.2 has reference to the second line of the stage direction at the beginning of the scene in question. A note on 115.1 has reference to the first line of the stage direction following line 115 of the text of the relevant scene. Speech prefixes, and any stage directions attached to them, are keyed to the first line of accompanying dialogue.

JOHN LOFTIS

Stanford University

Contents

List of Abbreviations

G	*Fatal Curiosity: A True Tragedy* .... London: Printed for John Gray, 1737. 8*vo*.
D1	*Fatal Curiosity* .... *The Second Edition.* London: Printed for T. Davies, 1762. 12*mo*.
A	*The Fatal Curiosity: An Affecting Narrative* .... London: Printed for O. Adams, 1768. 8*vo*.
D2	*The Works of Mr. George Lillo* .... London: Printed for T. Davies, 1775. 16*mo*.
H	*Fatal Curiosity* .... London: Printed for Harrison and Co., 1780. 8*vo*.
C	*Fatal Curiosity* ... *With Alterations* [by George Colman]. London: Printed for T. Cadell, 1783. 8*vo*.
om.	omitted
S.D.	stage direction
S.P.	speech prefix

Introduction

On May 27, 1736, Henry Fielding, manager of the Little Theatre in the Haymarket, presented a new tragedy by George Lillo entitled *Guilt Its Own Punishment; or, Fatal Curiosity.* The play was printed in 1737 as *Fatal Curiosity: A True Tragedy* . . . for John Gray, the official publisher of Lillo's works during the dramatist's lifetime. It was not reissued in England[1] until 1740, when it appeared in *The Works of the Late Mr. George Lillo.*[2] In 1762 Thomas Davies published "The Second Edition" with some minor verbal changes. Four years later, a production of the play at the Smock-Alley Theatre in Dublin occasioned an Irish edition, printed by and for Adams and Hyder. This 1766 version included substantial revisions in the third act, which may explain why Adams calls himself "the Proprietor" and warns of penalties for piracy in a "Seventh Edition" printed at Leeds in 1767 and at London in 1768.[3] Undeterred by Adams's alleged ownership, Davies included *Fatal Curiosity* in his *The Works of Mr. George Lillo* (1775). This was followed in 1780 by an edition printed for Harrison and Company.[4]

[1] There was an Irish edition in 1737, printed for A. Bradly, Dublin, and J. Potts, Belfast. Dr. James G. McManaway of the Folger Shakespeare Library says that this Dublin copy is a variant of the London 1737 edition, differing only in the wording of the imprint, and he suggests that both title pages may have been printed in London with this single stop-press change.

[2] This collection was also printed for John Gray. The title page and contents of *Fatal Curiosity* are identical with those of Gray's edition of 1737, London.

[3] Orion Adams (1726–1797), an itinerant printer who is known to have worked in Dublin, Manchester, Chester, Plymouth, and London. To the Leeds edition he appended *A Letter From the Unfortunate and Famous Sir Walter Ralegh to his Lady* . . . , and to the London edition he prefixed *The Young Lady's Preceptor; or Letters To a Young Lady of Distinction, upon Politeness* . . . . In the latter edition Adams declares that "the great success in the sale for this curious piece, both in England and Ireland, is almost incredible, this being the sixth edition in one year." Unless he was counting now-lost provincial publications, the figure is dubious.

[4] The 1775 Davies edition follows the original Gray text more closely

Between 1782 and 1784 two rival adaptations of the tragedy, by George Colman the elder and Henry Mackenzie, appeared on London stages and bookstalls. Eventually, the Colman text (1783) surpassed in popularity not only Mackenzie's version[5] but also Lillo's original. Bell's *British Theatre* (1797) and the second edition of Davies's *Works of Mr. George Lillo* (1810) remained faithful to the 1737 text, but editions in 1808, 1811, 1824, 1826, and 1864 accepted Colman's changes.[6]

The original 1737 Gray publication has been used as the copy-text for this edition. I have collated the first two editions printed for Davies, since he acted in the first production of the play and may have recalled changes made by Lillo during rehearsals;[7] the Adams version, since it was the first to alter the conclusion; the Harrison version, which Colman seems to have followed; and Colman's adaptation, which became the form most familiar to nineteenth-century readers. Mackenzie's alterations and expansion will be discussed later in the introduction, but it seems undesirable to record them in the textual notes. In presenting Lillo's text I have modernized punctuation, capitalization, and spelling. I have retained contractions, however, and have arranged divided lines typographically to show the blank verse form. In a few places Lillo's metrical intentions are not clear; I have indicated these passages in the textual notes.

During its first season in the spring of 1736, *Fatal Curiosity* was presented seven times. This, as Thomas Davies later remarked, was "very little success," and he blamed the relative failure on the poor taste of the managers of the two patent theaters, who preferred pomp and pantomime or buffoons and boxers:

> It is not easy to guess why this excellent piece was not represented at one of the Theatres Royal, as our author's character as a writer was by this time well established. It cannot be

---

than does the 1762 Davies, and Harrison appears to have used the 1762 Davies edition rather than the more recent publication of 1775. Both Davies and Harrison ignore the Adams revisions.

[5] Apparently Mackenzie's *The Shipwreck; or, Fatal Curiosity* (London, 1784) had only one edition.

[6] These are all in collections of English plays.

[7] "It was during the rehearsal of the *Fatal Curiosity* that I had an opportunity to see and converse with Mr. Lillo" (*The Works of Mr. George Lillo: with Some Account of his Life* [London: Printed for T. Davies, 1775], I, xvi).

> doubted that Lillo applied to the managers of the more regular theatres, and had been rejected, so that he was reduced to the necessity of having his play acted at an inferior Play-house, and by persons not so well skilled in their profession as the players of the established Theatres.[8]

However, Fielding, who had "a just sense of [the] author's merit,"[9] undertook to remedy these initial defects by directing the play, instructing the actors (Davies among them), and providing it with a new afterpiece, his own highly provocative *Historical Register for 1736.*[10] Thus refurbished, *Fatal Curiosity* returned to the stage in March, 1737 and ran for eleven nights. Ironically, Lillo's close association with Fielding may have been to some extent a cause for the sudden eclipse of the play. It was last given during that season on May 2, 1737. On June 2 the Stage Licensing Act was read to Parliament, and on June 21 the Act received royal assent. Fielding withdrew from the theater, Lillo lost both champion and stage, and the tragedy was not presented again before his death in 1739.

Although *Fatal Curiosity* suffered from this unfortunate theatrical coincidence, the piece does not seem to have pleased the public any more than it had the managers of the patent playhouses. Revived briefly in 1741 and once in 1742, it was ignored until 1755, when it was given as a benefit for Mrs. Charlotte Charke, the original Agnes. Its later record was equally sporadic. John Genest lists nine or ten performances of Colman's version in 1782; a noteworthy revival in 1797 with Mrs. Sarah Siddons, her father, and her brother as Agnes, Old Wilmot, and Randal; and one presentation in 1808.[11] His account concludes with a description of a performance at Bath in 1813 which was stopped by the audience.[12]

[8] *Ibid.*, I, xxxv. Davies also suggested that it may have suffered from "being brought on in the latter end of the season, when the public had been satiated with a long run of Pasquins."

[9] *Ibid.*, I, xv.

[10] In 1736 the afterpiece had been Fielding's *Tumble Down Dick; or, Phaeton in the Suds.*

[11] *Some Account of the English Stage from the Restoration in 1660 to 1830* (Bath, 1832), *passim.*

[12] "Fatal Curiosity was revived with an additional scene, which Lillo is said to have added to some edition of his play . . . . Young Wilmot entered in a dying state, after he had been stabbed by his father—this was thought by some too shocking—and the play was not suffered to be finished" (*ibid.*, VIII, 388).

In view of the phenomenal success of *The London Merchant* during the eighteenth century,[13] the immediate and lasting neglect of *Fatal Curiosity* is puzzling, for it has many of the popular attractions of the earlier play. The plot was based on a crime reported in a pamphlet, *Newes from Perin in Cornwall of A most Bloody and un-exampled Murther* . . . (1618) and repeated as fact in the respectable annals of Sanderson and Frankland.[14] It could, therefore, be considered a "true" tragedy by the middle-class spectator.[15] As in *The London Merchant*, trade and patriotism are jointly praised. Young Wilmot has "improved, by care and honest commerce, [his] little stock," and has returned with his wealth to England,[16] the "seat of plenty, liberty, and health." His boyhood companion, Randal, is an upright young Englishman who plans to claim "the fair inheritance of ev'ry Briton" in a search for fortune overseas; and his friend, Eustace, thriftily denounces "idle pomp and luxury." Linked to these mercantile ideals is, again, anti-Spanish sentiment occasioned by trade rivalry, a topic of great interest in both Court and City circles in 1736.[17]

Although Charles Lamb called *The London Merchant* a "nauseous sermon,"[18] its pervasive didacticism was the result of Lillo's belief that "the more extensively useful the moral of any tragedy is, the more excellent that piece must be of its kind."[19] Certainly the

[13] Emmett L. Avery estimates that it was staged 179 times between 1731 and 1776 ("The Popularity of *The Mourning Bride* in the London Theaters in the Eighteenth Century," *Research Studies of the State College of Washington*, IX [1941], 115–116).

[14] See Appendix B.

[15] Whether or not the Cornish crime occurred has been questioned, since Austrian, Bohemian, German, Italian, Corsican, Bulgarian, Polish, and Chinese analogues have been found. See William E. A. Axon, "The Story of Lillo's 'Fatal Curiosity,'" *Notes & Queries*, 6th Series, V (1882), 21–23.

[16] "It is the industrious merchant's business to collect the various blessings of each soil and climate, and, with the product of the whole, to enrich his native country" (*The London Merchant*, III.i).

[17] The apparently irrelevant account of Ralegh's return and of Spanish insolence parallels the opening conversation in *The London Merchant* concerning the delay of the Armada. Here, however, more than topical purposes are served: the story of Ralegh's fate reinforces Old Wilmot's cynicism about the rewards of virtue, and Ralegh's betrayal by a kinsman upon his return from a search for gold foreshadows the fate of Young Wilmot.

[18] "On the Tragedies of Shakespeare," *The Works of Charles and Mary Lamb*, ed. E. V. Lucas (London, 1903), I, 102, n. 1.

[19] Dedication, *The London Merchant*, 1731.

campaign "to refine the age/ To chasten wit, and moralize the stage,"[20] reflected in the works of Steele and others, had Lillo's complete support. In *Fatal Curiosity* he preached the virtues of filial piety, charity to orphans, respect of servants for masters, self-reliance, and, above all, patient submission to the will of God. His contemporaries who praised *The London Merchant* as an "instructive, moral, and cautionary drama"[21] should have found similarities to it in *Fatal Curiosity*. And by adding the character of Charlot to the original plot, Lillo gratified the growing taste for sentimentality. To some extent Charlot resembles the lovelorn Maria in *The London Merchant*, but she is more carefully developed and more genuinely pathetic. The song of her maid-confidante contributed both pathos and fashionable entertainment.[22]

Persons of learning must also have realized that by an extensive overlay of echoes from earlier drama Lillo had again, and more successfully, attempted to elevate a simple, sensational plot to the level of art. Fielding declared that *Fatal Curiosity* was "a Master-Piece of its kind and inferior only to Shakespear's best pieces."[23] This judgment was repeated by Sarah Fielding, Thomas Davies, James Harris, George Colman, and James Boaden. Although eighteenth-century critics tended to be prodigal in finding playwrights who were "next to Shakespeare," one of the outstanding features of Lillo's tragedy is, in fact, his use of Shakespearean material, particularly *Macbeth*. He had shown some skill in adapting the famous murder scene for *The London Merchant*. But in *Fatal Curiosity* the borrowing is so detailed that few could have failed to note the parallels, from Agnes's fierce determination to obtain the fortune by "th'inhospitable murder of our guest," to her husband's cry, "Sleep those who may." Agnes has been dismissed as "a bourgeois Lady Macbeth,"[24] but such a transformation was, in part, Lillo's aim.

In the same way, Old Wilmot's meditations on life and death invite comparisons with *Hamlet*, as does Agnes's catalogue of "the whips and

[20] Prologue, *The Conscious Lovers*, 1722.

[21] Theophilus Cibber, *The Lives of the Poets of Great-Britain and Ireland* (London, 1753), V, 340.

[22] Lillo may have written the song for Miss Karver, who played the original Maria and was well known as a singer. In some later versions the song is omitted, and Maria becomes a "servant" or a "maid."

[23] *The Champion*, February 26, 1740.

[24] Reino Virtanen, "Camus' *Le Malentendu* and some Analogues," *Comparative Literature*, X (1958), 234.

scorns of time" at the beginning of the third act. Both Polonius and Lear may have contributed to Old Wilmot's opening scene with Randal. Young Wilmot, garbed like "a sun-burnt Indian," telling of his "strange escapes/ and perilous adventures" must have, visually and verbally, recalled to audiences Othello with his "moving accidents" and "hair-breadth 'scapes," which included a similar period of slavery. To complicate allusions, Young Wilmot's tales are to be "the theme/ Of many a happy winter night," and Charlot's remark, "There's sure no passion in the human soul/ But finds its food in music," may be based on the opening of *Twelfth Night*.

The spirit of "tender Otway" is often invoked. Essentially, the financial plight of the Wilmots is that of Jaffeir and Belvidera in *Venice Preserved*—bankruptcy[25] brought on by "wasteful riots," which were abetted by "pamper'd vermin" of servants.[26] Old Wilmot's misanthropy was anticipated in milder terms by Acasto in *The Orphan*, and throughout Lillo's play there are Otwavian personifications of poverty and want. Even more striking is Charlot's dream, which, in its mixture of sentimentality and sensuality, echoes various speeches of Belvidera.

According to the *Daily Advertiser* for May 28, 1736, the emotional scenes "were so artfully work'd up, and so well perform'd that there scarce remain'd a dry Eye among the Spectators at the Representation." Theophilus Cibber reported a similar tearful reception of the first performance of *The London Merchant*.[27] The account in the *Daily Advertiser* continues: "During the Scene preceding the Catastrophe, an attentive Silence possess'd the whole House, more expressive of an universal Approbation than the loudest Applause." This behavior, unusual for an early eighteenth-century audience, may have been an expression of approval, but it also seems an ominous prediction of future reactions to the play. It was seldom seen on the stage, and in 1775 Davies bluntly stated: "This tragedy is I believe little known."[28]

Between 1780 and 1830, however, there were at least ten printed versions. *Fatal Curiosity* had found a receptive public as closet drama. For this belated *succès d'estime*, the *Philological Inquiries* of James

[25] The bankruptcy is made explicit by Mackenzie in *The Shipwreck* (1784), but he ascribes it to excessive benevolence.

[26] "Discharge the lazy vermin of thy Hall/ Those Pageants of thy Folly" (Priuli to Jaffeir, *Venice Preserved*, I.i.105–106).

[27] Cibber, *Lives*, V, 340.

[28] *Works*, I, xvii.

Harris,[29] published in 1781, was largely responsible. Dr. Johnson called Harris "a prig, and a bad prig," but both Goldsmith and Boswell praised him as worthy, learned, "and in particular an eminent Grecian." As might be expected from a Greek scholar, Harris read *Fatal Curiosity* with classical tragedy in mind. Arguing from fairly regular Aristotelian principles,[30] he found Lillo's play to be "the model of a *Perfect Fable*," to reflect perfect manners (the characters have "a *suitable Consistence*"), and to have ideal dramatic sentiments ("the universal Subjects of our Discourse"). He declared that the tragedy, except in its diction, was the peer of *Othello*, *Lear*, *Samson Agonistes*, and the *Oedipus* of Sophocles. He insisted upon this last parallel, and in his commentary shrewdly pointed out elements of the play which had not been appreciated earlier. Not only was it Shakespearean; it was also classical in form and effect. In particular, he stressed Lillo's use of pity, terror, and horror, emotions which English readers, following Burke,[31] had increasingly come to regard as sources of the sublime. The reference to *Samson Agonistes*, which Harris felt had a similar "striking Revolution," is perhaps the most interesting of his insights, since Lillo was undoubtedly familiar with Milton's attempt to combine classical tragic form with Christian doctrine.

Harris's praise of *Fatal Curiosity* is enthusiastic and even extravagant: "What a Discovery! What a Revolution! How irresistibly are the *Tragic* Passions of *Terror* and *Pity* excited!"[32] Among those excited to re-examine the play were George Colman, manager of the Haymarket Theatre, and Henry Mackenzie, the Scottish novelist. Both decided that, with alterations, it would be suitable dramatic fare. Mackenzie later intimated that Colman had stolen the idea of such revision from him.[33] Whatever the truths of this minor theatrical

[29] Known as "Hermes" Harris for his *Hermes, or a Philosophical Inquiry Concerning Universal Grammar* (London, 1751), he was a gentleman-scholar of Salisbury and former member of Parliament. Although not a member of The Club, he was acquainted with Sir Joshua Reynolds and others, as well as with Mrs. Thrale.

[30] Harris believed that "the true Tragic Passions" are occasioned only by people of "middle" rank, who do not have extraordinary virtue.

[31] *A Philosophical Enquiry into the Origin of Our Ideas of the Sublime and the Beautiful* appeared in 1757.

[32] *Philological Inquiries* (London, 1781), p. 158.

[33] "The idea of this alteration of Lillo's *Fatal Curiosity* was first conceived from a perusal of the late Mr. Harris's Philological Essays, published in

war, Colman won by a year. His *Fatal Curiosity* was performed in 1782 and published in 1783; Mackenzie's version, *The Shipwreck*, reached stage and press in 1784.

In the extensive Irish revision of 1767, Adams had altered the last act to make Old Wilmot less ready to follow Agnes's murderous design and had added as a conclusion a full-blown mad scene for Charlot. Colman, however, shortened the role of Charlot in the third act, cutting out her speech beginning "This is the third time those fantastic forms," as well as her final entry, in which she is supported by Maria and Randal. Agnes's report to the audience of the off-stage murder is shortened and revised "to correct; and even in some measure to mitigate the horror of the catastrophe, by the omission of some expressions rather too savage, and by one or two touches of remorse and tenderness."[34] Following Harris's advice "totally to expunge those *wretched Rhimes*, which conclude many of the Scenes, and which 'tis probable are not from Lillo,"[35] Colman removed all the couplets except one which he thought "too beautiful to be displaced."[36] He also omitted the long passage dealing with the fate of Sir Walter Ralegh in the first act. Other changes are mainly verbal—substitutions for words, phrases, and lines which seemed unacceptable to later eighteenth-century taste. The effect is that of reducing an already short tragedy by one-sixth of its original length.[37] The reasons for the excisions are not hard to find: Colman did not understand Lillo's intention in the use of the couplets; he felt that Anglo-Spanish trade rivalry was no longer of general interest; and, by reducing Charlot's role, he could achieve a clearer focus on the tragedy of the elder Wilmots.

If Colman cut the play in an effort to mitigate the horror of Agnes's savagery, Mackenzie attempted to provide "a better apology

---

1780. It was communicated to Mr. Colman, by a friend of the Author's, Spring 1782; but it seems Mr. Colman had, at that time, by a singular coincidence of sentiments, resolved to bring out Lillo's play at his theatre, which he accordingly did the ensuing Summer" ("Advertisement," *The Shipwreck: or, Fatal Curiosity* [London: Printed for T. Cadell, 1784]).

[34] Postscript, *Fatal Curiosity . . . With Alterations* (London: Printed for T. Cadell, 1783), p. 47.

[35] *Philological Inquiries*, p. 172.

[36] Postscript, *Fatal Curiosity*, p. 48.

[37] Lillo's play has 1244 lines, the Colman version 1050 lines. For comparison one may cite *Macbeth* (2210 lines), Addison's *Cato* (1900 lines), and Home's *Douglas* (1705 lines). All figures are approximate.

for Wilmot's commission of the crime."[38] To accomplish this, he expanded the play from three to five acts. Old Wilmot is transmuted into a good-natured man of feeling who has been ruined by his generosity. Lillo's vague threat of destitution is made real in the person of a villainous former steward who has become an attorney and is literally at the door with a foreclosure notice. A grandson, by a now-dead daughter, is introduced to prattle winningly about a freezing robin in the manner of Thomson's *Winter* and to talk piteously about the sufferings which he and his grandparents must soon endure.[39] Mackenzie's prologue announced that "the Author of to-night/ From Lillo's perch has try'd a little flight." His flight was happily of short duration, and *Fatal Curiosity*, in any form, had to wait for the brief Siddons revival of 1797.

Meanwhile, the play continued to be read, as the repeated printings indicate. Mrs. Elizabeth Inchbald included it in her influential collection, *The British Theatre* (London, 1808), using the Colman version. In the "Biographical and Critical Remarks" she praises it highly, but there is an undertone of reservation. The play requires "a reader, of good taste, and strong nerves," since "for want of that robust constitution just alluded to, which implies strength of mind as well as body, an audience shrinks from beholding it performed."[40] This may be an oblique tribute to her own bluestocking good taste and strong nerves, for she continues with an account of an actual performance at which, in the third act, "a certain horror seized the audience, and was manifested by a kind of stifled scream."[41]

[38] James Boaden, who saw the actors Bensley and Henderson play the role of Old Wilmot in the Colman and Mackenzie versions, respectively, reports the different emotional effects: "The act [of murder] excited less *surprise* from Bensley, and the sympathy for *him* was therefore less; but he was terrible and even sublime. Henderson had our love from his first line, and the distress was, perhaps, greater, that so noble a nature should be thus ensnared to his perdition" (*Memoirs of Mrs. Siddons* . . . [London, 1827], p. 270).

[39] The boy's role was originally played by a Miss Heard. Mackenzie explained that the addition was intended "not only to infuse somewhat more of pity into the calamity of the Wilmot family, but to give an opportunity of shewing the distresses resulting from their poverty, on which the pride and delicacy of a more advanced age do not easily allow it to develope" ("Advertisement," *The Shipwreck*).

[40] XI, iii.

[41] XI, v. Thomas Campbell reports a similar reaction to Lillo's *Arden of Feversham*, first produced in 1762: "The audience rose up with one accord and interrupted it" (*Specimens of the British Poets* [London, 1819], V, 59).

Continental readers and spectators were evidently more sturdy. Even before the Colman and Mackenzie versions were presented, Karl Philipp Moritz wrote an imitation of *Fatal Curiosity* entitled *Blunt oder der Gast, Schauspiel in einem Akt*, which was published in Berlin in 1781. W. H. Brömel's translation, *Stolz und Verzweiflung*,[42] had editions in 1785 and 1791. Lillo's plot was also employed by Zacharias Werner in *Der Vierundzwanzigste Februar* (1812), by Adolf Mülner in *Der Neunundzwanzigste Februar* and *Die Schuld* (both in 1812), and at some distance by Franz Grillparzer in *Die Ahnfrau* (1817). Indirect influence on Lessing and Schiller is possible.[43]

Thus Lillo's tragedy was assimilated into an important branch of early nineteenth-century German drama. Yet the association has done *Fatal Curiosity* a disservice. Later critics, such as Adolphus W. Ward, have tended to see the English play only as "an early experiment in a species to which the Germans, who alone cultivated it to any considerable extent, have given the name of *Schicksaltragödie* . . . [a species] not introducing a new element into tragedy but exaggerating in various degrees of grotesqueness . . . an element which in itself is foreign neither to ancient nor to modern tragedy." Ward continues: "Lillo, whether consciously or not, in his *Fatal Curiosity* took a step which may be regarded as transnormal: not because in the narrow work of his domestic tragedy he once more pictured *la fuerza del destino* . . . but because, in point of fact, he exhibited destiny as operating to all intents and purposes independently of character . . . . The effect of this tragedy is therefore as hollow as it is horrible."[44]

From the grotesque to the absurd is an easy step. In 1958 Reino Virtanen discussed *Le Malentendu* of Albert Camus and some analogues, including Werner's *Der Vierundzwanzigste Februar* and *Fatal Curiosity*. The French play, he correctly asserts, is "not a simple derivative from Lillo,"[45] and, possibly echoing Ward, he denounces

[42] This title may have been taken from Randal's concluding speech in the Colman version: "Bear hence/ These bleeding victims of despair and pride."

[43] Henry Crabbe Robinson discussed Lillo's works with Schiller, who often employed "fate" motifs in his plays. Schiller expressed admiration for *The London Merchant* but denied having read *Fatal Curiosity* (Robinson, *Diary* [London, 1869], I, 213).

[44] *The London Merchant or the History of George Barnwell and Fatal Curiosity* (Boston and London, 1906), pp. 1–liii.

[45] Virtanen, "Camus' *Le Malentendu*," pp. 233–234. It should be noted that Camus was familiar with Defoe's *Journal of the Plague Year*, as *La Peste*

the "hollowness" of *Fatal Curiosity*: Young Wilmot "comes to his disaster through the contrivance of an author heedless of verisimilitude and intent on producing effects of horror which he dilutes with pietistic moralizing."[46]

Revised in the latter part of the eighteenth century to conform with pre-Romantic English tastes, rejected in 1906 as a forerunner of German dramatic aberration, and found wanting by a defender of French existentialist drama, Lillo's play has, at least, proven its controversial value. As Genest remarked from Bath in 1832: "This T. is peculiarly interesting."[47]

The peculiar interest of the tragedy remains, but it must be understood in the terms of Lillo and his time. Henry Fielding said that *Fatal Curiosity* gave Lillo "a title to be call'd the best Tragic Poet of his Age" and eulogized him as having "the Spirit of an old *Roman*, joined to the Innocence of a primitive Christian."[48] He thus provided a key to Lillo's dramatic purpose, which was a combination of the classical and the Christian. That Lillo was a middle-class Dissenter who was esteemed as a person of "unblemished character [and] strict morals"[49] has become a traditional statement in literary histories. That he was well-read, despite the lack of a university education, is seldom mentioned. Yet the sale catalogue for his library, printed after his death in 1739, presents evidence that he was familiar not only with Elizabethan, Jacobean, and "Modern Dramatick Writers," but also with Euripedes, Sophocles, and, particularly, Seneca.[50]

As James Harris realized, *Fatal Curiosity*, despite the humble origins of its plot, has many affinities with classical drama. The dramatic unities are more rigidly observed than they are in Addison's "regular" tragedy, *Cato*, which Lillo admired.[51] Instead of progressing from overcast dawn to sunset of the fatal day, Lillo begins his play in late afternoon and concludes it with such economy that acting time and plot time are almost identical. All three settings are confined to the

shows, and that he took the epigraph for that novel from the preface to the third, and relatively unread, volume of *Robinson Crusoe*. Excursions into other early eighteenth-century works cannot be proven but are not unlikely.

46 *Ibid.*, p. 234.

47 *Some Account of the English Stage*, III, 489.

48 *The Champion*, February 26, 1740.

49 Cibber, *Lives*, V, 338.

50 See my article, "What George Lillo Read: A Speculation," *Huntington Library Quarterly*, XXIX (May, 1966), 275–286.

51 Dedication, *The London Merchant*.

town of Penryn; and, since Charlot has been the mainstay of the elder Wilmots during her fiancé's absence, the love plot does not mar unity of action as it does in *Cato*. Several speeches, such as Charlot's dream and Young Wilmot's account of his supposed death and wandering ghost, are set pieces in the classical manner. The actual death takes place off-stage, with Agnes serving as narrator. The rhyming conclusions of the seven scenes are vestiges of sententious choruses which comment on past and future action.[52]

Racine, Lee, Dryden, Addison, and others had adapted classical material to contemporary tastes. Southerne and Rowe had shown that "a tale . . . told long since" could with "strength and nature make amends for art."[53] Lillo in *The London Merchant* had tried to accommodate tragedy "to the circumstances of the generality of mankind."[54] In *Fatal Curiosity* his ambitious project was to show that material which was unquestionably English and outside the realm of fustian heroes could also be fitted into the form of classical tragedy.

How well he succeeded with this plan is debatable. Mrs. Inchbald remarked that his earlier work "gives not even an intimation that the same dramatist could ever arrive to that degree of perfection in his art, as to produce *Fatal Curiosity*."[55] To understand the extravagance of the praise, we must understand the conventions within which Lillo was working, including the convention of the double title, which had been fashionable in both comedy and tragedy since 1660. The first title stated a norm or a problem, and the second implied or stated a complementary aspect of the problem. Thus, in *Guilt Its Own Punishment; or, Fatal Curiosity*,[56] Lillo suggests that Old Wilmot and Agnes, who commit "this horrid deed that punishes itself," are complemented by their son, whose "curiosity" brings disaster to himself and to his parents.

52 These couplets are crucial to an interpretation of the tragedy and their metaphors are adroitly consistent. Randal and Charlot first prophesy the fates of Old Wilmot and Agnes in the ruined-temple and blasted-tree comparisons. Young Wilmot then closes four successive scenes with predictions of his own doom, and Randal concludes the tragedy by urging submission to the will of God.

53 Prologue, *The Tragedy of Jane Shore*, ll. 3, 20.

54 Dedication, *The London Merchant*.

55 *The British Theatre*, XI, iv.

56 The title was reduced to *Fatal Curiosity* after the first performance, perhaps in imitation of those of such plays as *The Fatal Dowry* and *The Fatal Marriage*.

Old Wilmot is the real protagonist of the tragedy, a complex character "chequered with Good and with Evil."[57] His servant says that he is honorable, charitable, and considerate. His wife, in her conversation with Charlot and even in her dying remark, indicates that he is a fond, almost uxorious husband. From his son's inability to decide "of two so dear which I could bear to lose," we might assume that he had been a good father. The initial impression is that of a perfect patriarch, now fallen upon evil days and suffering undeserved misery. However, from the same sources, another picture emerges. Randal also says that Old Wilmot is imprudent, pleasure-loving, and proud. Agnes expands these hints when, in self-defense, she denounces his luxurious pride which has led him to squander their estate, including her dowry, in "wasteful riots." The loving son has been sent to "some remote, inhospitable land" to restore the family fortunes while the "unnat'ral father" remains at home, living on Charlot's charity and reading Seneca's maxims on the blessings of poverty.

The self-indulgence of Old Wilmot, however, is venial compared with the sins Lillo reveals during the course of the play. Intellectual pride, increased by philosophical studies without the counterbalance of Christian faith, has caused him to doubt Divine Providence. His attempts to corrupt Randal's mind with his cynicism and to involve Agnes in his blasphemous scheme of suicide show him to have become actively evil. Ward is correct in saying that "the demoralizing effects of want and 'dire necessity' upon Old Wilmot and his wife are of course quite insufficient to account for the sophistry with which she 'seduces his will' and 'infects his soul' so as to secure his connivance in her criminal design."[58] In *The London Merchant* Lillo strained psychological probability with his condensed presentation of the innocent apprentice's temptation, decline, and fall, but Old Wilmot has already fallen before the curtain rises on the symbolic sunset which follows the "fatal tempest" and his son's shipwreck. Hope, he says, is "vain, flattering, delusive, groundless," and the distinction between "the less or greater" crime has become meaningless in the general collapse of reason and the triumph of proud despair. Sanderson's *Compleat History*[59] attributed Old Wilmot's fall to his wife's "puling fondness (Eve's enchantment)." There are similarities to the

[57] Harris, *Philological Inquiries*, p. 171.
[58] Ward, *The London Merchant*, p. liii.
[59] See Appendix B.

Biblical and Miltonic Adam and Eve, but, as Randal suggests early in the play, Old Wilmot is a damned soul before the murder, "a majestic temple sunk to ruin/ . . . the loathsome shelter and abode/ Of lurking serpents."

Whereas his tragic flaw is one of misused intellect, that of Agnes, symbolized by her "faded dress unfashionably fine" and the "strained complaisance" of her manners, is social pride. To this fault must be added ingratitude, lack of Christian resignation, anger, and a flaunting of the controls of reason. Old Wilmot is "my wretched husband," "my poor husband," "cruel husband," and, as alternate passions move her, "ever kind" husband. Guided only by emotion, her heart is quickly ravished by the sight of "the bright temptation" and, as quickly, she implements her desires with the first instrument that comes to hand. The deed is "not to be thought on," and her arguments are as glib as Old Wilmot's musings about man's fate are ponderous. In many ways she is an obvious antithesis of her husband. However, Lillo's intentions in characterizing her are complex. Possibly recalling Jocasta's contempt of oracles,[60] he has her scoff twice at the dream which Charlot believes may be an "admonition of a friendly power." Like her husband, Agnes proudly rejects the possibility of a Providence beyond her control and in turn prophesies: "'Tis just as likely Wilmot should return/ As we become your foe."

Here again, social vanity is mere folly in comparison with the darker sin of pride. Agnes sneers at her husband for not having prayed until the moment of the murder, but her ambiguous question of "What pow'r shall I invoke to aid thee, Wilmot?" is easily answered. And the attentive reader is less surprised than Agnes herself at the ease with which the fatal casket springs open. As Randal had lamented the "horrid transformation" of Old Wilmot at the end of the first act, so, at the end of the second, Young Wilmot comments on the change in his mother's "lovely form and mind" that makes him "dread I know not what."

The care with which Lillo created the elder Wilmots is paralleled in his treatment of the son. Critics have acknowledged similarities to the fatal curiosity of Oedipus but have been inclined to excuse

[60] The catalogue of Lillo's library listed a *History of Oracles* (1688). Harris praised Lillo for not using "Machines, Deities, Prodigies, Spectres, or any thing else, incomprehensible or incredible" (*Philological Inquiries*, p. 157). Charlot's dream does, however, serve some of the purposes of the Delphic oracle in *Oedipus*.

Young Wilmot as a callow, mischievous, yet virtuous boy. If he is indeed such an innocent victim of Fate, the play is "a tragic farce/ Tedious though short, and without art elab'rate/ Ridiculously sad."[61] As a Christian and as a Dissenter, Lillo could not have subscribed to this view. Destiny is in action, but it is not "operating to all intents and purposes independently of character."[62]

Young Wilmot is first presented as a paragon—a young man of physical endurance and courage, a resourceful and honest merchant, an ardent patriot, dutiful son, faithful lover, and loyal friend. Two flaws in his character are, however, soon apparent: the classic sin of *hubris* in his presumption of continuing good fortune, and a luxurious sensibility which leads him to exploit the extremes of sensation. He is, thus, the true son of Old Wilmot, whose intellectual pride has led him to a presumption of continuing *ill* fortune, and of Agnes, who is controlled by her passions. His many escapes from "savage men" have resulted in a false sense of security which must, nevertheless, be tested by a manipulation of events in order to "refine on happiness." This curiosity is not a boyish prank but a tampering with Divine Providence. Such "trial" scenes as that with Charlot had often been used in tragicomedy; here the effect is unpleasant since it reveals the depths of Young Wilmot's self-indulgence. He has been told that she is still "as true as fair," but he cruelly forces her into tearful protestations of her fidelity. A similar test of his parents is prevented only by the self-inflicted emotions of "superfluous pain" and "fondness."

The death cry, "Oh, Father! Father!" is pathetic, but Young Wilmot is no Iphigenia or Isaac, sacrificed on the altar of his father's necessity. Instead, he is his own victim; in one final and fatal gamble (to "multiply my joys"), he puts himself and his fortune into the hands of "wretches mad with anguish" and "unthinking, furnished [them] with arms against himself."[63] His parents, whom he so much resembles, ironically become his victims.

Lillo's dark vision of human nature is not unrelieved. Goodness is clearly represented in the secondary characters. Charlot is the exemplar of patience, constancy, and resignation—a foil for the

[61] *Fatal Curiosity*, I.i.16–18. [62] Ward, *The London Merchant*, p. liii.

[63] In Camus' *L'Étranger*, Mersault reads a newspaper account of a similar murder and remarks: "D'un côté elle était invraisemblable. D'un autre, elle était naturelle. De toute façon, je trouvais que le voyageur l'avait un peu merité et qu'il ne faut jamais jouer." Camus expands this idea—that one should never gamble with Fate—in his play, *Le Malentendu*.

cynical Maria and the "cruel, remorseless, and impatient" Agnes. Randal, with his simple love and diligence, balances the misanthropy of Old Wilmot, the Stoic turned Machiavel. Randal also serves as a pious counterpart of Young Wilmot when he tries to dissuade him from the forged letter and reproves his "boundless curiosity." Eustace is an undeveloped reworking of George Barnwell's friend, Trueman, and an even more shadowy version of the conventional "friend" of heroic drama. However, he is given the Sophoclean key lines to the play:

> Blind to events, we reason in the dark,
> And fondly apprehend what none e'er found
> Or ever shall: pleasure and pain unmixed.
> And flatter, and torment ourselves, by turns
> With what shall never be.

Randal, the ingénu and "honest wretch" of the opening scene, delivers the final choral speech, which in its somberness is worthy of Old Wilmot. Using a sunset metaphor deriving from the tragic action, he declares:

> Though youthful Wilmot's sun be set ere noon,
> The ripe in virtue never die too soon.

This epitaph, perhaps intended as an ironic version of "Quem Di diligunt, adolescens moritur,"[64] is matched by his pessimistic capping of Old Wilmot's last line, which ends in Shakespearean fashion with an interrupted perception: "Mankind may learn—but—oh!" To which Randal adds with stark finality, "Most will not."[65]

Whatever its "terrible graces,"[66] *Fatal Curiosity* must have seemed a puzzling play to any thoughtful spectator in the eighteenth century. The modern reader, if he accepts it as more than an unmotivated exploitation of horror, may also have difficulty in discovering Lillo's theme in the mixture of pagan and Calvinistic doctrines, of classical and Shakespearean devices, which the dramatist imposed upon the framework of a Jacobean criminal pamphlet. No easy interpretation is possible.

Allardyce Nicoll praises *Fatal Curiosity* as the only tragic masterpiece produced between 1700 and 1750.[67] If so, the play was and has remained a singularly neglected masterpiece. Too "low" for Lillo's

[64] Plautus, *Bacchides*, IV.vii.
[65] Colman changed this remark to "Heaven grant they may."
[66] Davies, *Works*, I, xxvii.
[67] *A History of English Drama, 1660–1900* (Cambridge, 1952), II, 124.

contemporaries[68] and too nerve-wracking for later taste, it was not a popular success, even in revised form. The topical appeals faded. The conventions of structure and speech familiar to Fielding's theater in the Haymarket became outmoded. The blank verse, despite its many literary echoes, ceased to linger in the minds of readers.[69]

As in the case of *The London Merchant*, the psychological insights which Lillo attempted to embody in compact dramatic form found more extended expression in the emerging English novel. Richardson wrote his version of a Christian tragedy in *Clarissa*. Fielding used the Stoic–Christian debate as a basis for *Amelia*.[70] The works of Sterne, Goldsmith, and Mackenzie variously illustrated the pleasures and perils of indulging emotions. And the more sensational aspects of Lillo's play, such as the thrice-repeated monitory dream, the unwitting filicide, and the sepulchral off-stage groans became stock incidents in the Gothic romances of Walpole and Radcliffe.

Despite its faults, *Fatal Curiosity* "stamps Lillo as being a genius of no common rank."[71] Appearing in 1736, just before the Stage Licensing Act, it is an interesting landmark in English literary history—at once a climax to Restoration tragedy written according to "the rules," and a dramatic protest against the "frigid caution" of an age in which "Declamation roar'd whilst Passion slept."[72]

WILLIAM H. MCBURNEY

University of Illinois

[68] A group of ladies in Sarah Fielding's *The Adventures of David Simple* (Book II, Chapter 2) discusses Lillo's works caustically: "Certainly that fellow must be something very low, for his distresses always arise from poverty; and then he brings his wicked wretches, who are to be tempted for money to some monstrous action, which he would have his audience pity them for."

[69] Thomas Campbell in *Specimens of the British Poets* (London, 1819), V, 59–60, discusses this lack: "Notwithstanding the power of Lillo's works, we entirely miss in them that romantic attraction which invites repeated perusal of them. They give us life in a close and dreadful semblance of reality, but not arrayed in the magic illusion of poetry. His strength lies in conception of situations, not in beauty of dialogue or in the eloquence of the passions." Bonamy Dobrée calls the blank verse "workmanlike but unstirring" (*English Literature in the Early Eighteenth Century, 1700–1740* [Oxford, 1959], p. 254).

[70] See George Sherburn, "Fielding's *Amelia*: An Interpretation," *Journal of English Literary History*, III (1936), 1–14.

[71] Nicoll, *History of English Drama*, II, 122.

[72] Samuel Johnson, "Prologue Spoken by Mr. Garrick at the Opening of the Theatre Royal, Drury Lane, 1747," ll. 31–32.

FATAL CURIOSITY

PROLOGUE

Written by Henry Fielding, Esq.
Spoken by Mr. Roberts.

The Tragic Muse has long forgot to please
With Shakespeare's nature, or with Fletcher's ease.
No passion moved, through five long acts you sit,
Charmed with the poet's language, or his wit.
Fine things are said, no matter whence they fall; 5
Each single character might speak them all.
But from this modern fashionable way,
Tonight our author begs your leave to stray.
No fustian hero rages here tonight;
No armies fall to fix a tyrant's right. 10
From lower life we draw our scene's distress;
Let not your equals move your pity less!
Virtue distressed in humble state support,
Nor think she never lives without the Court.
Though to our scenes no royal robes belong, 15
And though our little stage as yet be young,
Throw both your scorn and prejudice aside;
Let us with favor, not contempt, be tried.
Through the first acts a kind attention lend;
The growing scene shall force you to attend, 20
Shall catch the eyes of every tender fair,

Fielding] *D1–C;* Feilding *G.*

---

1. *The . . . Muse*] This line seems to echo derisively the opening lines of the prologue to *The London Merchant,* which was spoken by Theophilus Cibber: "The Tragic Muse, sublime, delights to show."

3. *five . . . acts*] As a three-act play, *Fatal Curiosity* was a novelty in the 1730's.

14. *without the Court*] outside, beyond, or possibly without the example or support of the royal court.

16. *our . . . stage*] The Little, New, or French Theatre in the Haymarket, as it was variously known, opened in December, 1720, and was originally used by troupes of French comedians. After years of intermittent occupancy, it had again reopened in March, 1736, under Fielding's management with a performance of *Pasquin*. The *little stage* was therefore *young*. Its lack of a royal patent, early association with French actors, and generally checkered past explain Fielding's plea for tolerance.

And make them charm their lovers with a tear.
The lover, too, by pity shall impart
His tender passion to his fair one's heart.
The breast which others' anguish cannot move 25
Was ne'er the seat of friendship, or of love.

DRAMATIS PERSONAE

Men

OLD WILMOT	*Mr. Roberts*
YOUNG WILMOT	*Mr. Davis*
EUSTACE	*Mr. Wooburn*
RANDAL	*Mr. Blakes*

Women

AGNES, wife to Old Wilmot	*Mrs. Charke*
CHARLOT	*Miss Jones*
MARIA	*Miss Karver*

VISITORS, men and women

Scene: *Penryn in Cornwall*

Davis, Wooburn] *G;* Davies, Woodburn *D1, D2, C.; om. A, H.*

VISITORS] *D2, H;* Visiters *G, D1; om. A, C.*

Mr. Roberts, Mrs. Charke] They played the roles of Barnwell and Lucy in the original production of *The London Merchant.*

Penryn] a town at the head of Penryn Creek, which flows into the estuary of the Fal, about three miles from Falmouth.

Fatal Curiosity

ACT I

[I.i] *A room in Wilmot's house.*

OLD WILMOT (*alone*).

The day is far advanced. The cheerful sun
Pursues with vigor his repeated course,
No labor less'ning, nor no time decaying
His strength, or splendor. Evermore the same,
From age to age his influence sustains 5
Dependent worlds, bestows both life and motion
On the dull mass that forms their dusky orbs,
Cheers them with heat, and gilds them with his brightness.
Yet man, of jarring elements composed,
Who posts from change to change, from the first hour 10
Of his frail being till his dissolution,
Enjoys the sad prerogative above him:
To think, and to be wretched. What is life
To him that's born to die? Or what that wisdom
Whose perfection ends in knowing we know nothing? 15
Mere contradictions all! A tragic farce,
Tedious though short, and without art elab'rate,
Ridiculously sad—

Enter Randal.

Where hast been, Randal?

RANDAL.

Not out of Penryn, sir; but to the strand
To hear what news from Falmouth since the storm 20
Of wind last night.

3. less'ning] *G;* lessening *D2;* lessens *D1, A, H, C.*
3. decaying] *G, D2;* decays *D1, A, H, C.*
17. without art elab'rate] *G, A, D2;* elab'rate without art *D1, H, C.*

---

10. *posts*] hastens.

OLD WILMOT. It was a dreadful one.

RANDAL.

Some found it so. A noble ship from India,
Ent'ring in the harbor, run upon a rock,
And there was lost.

OLD WILMOT. What 'came of those on board her?

RANDAL.

Some few are saved, but much the greater part, 25
'Tis thought, are perished.

OLD WILMOT. They are past the fear
Of future tempests, or a wreck on shore.
Those who escaped are still exposed to both.

RANDAL.

But I've heard news much stranger than this shipwreck
Here in Cornwall. The brave Sir Walter Ralegh, 30
Being arrived at Plymouth from Guiana,
A most unhappy voyage, has been betrayed
By base Sir Lewis Stukeley, his own kinsman,
And seiz'd on by an order from the Court,
And 'tis reported he must lose his head 35
To satisfy the Spaniards.

OLD WILMOT. Not unlikely.
His martial genius does not suit the times.
There's now no insolence that Spain can offer
But, to the shame of this pacific reign,

23. Ent'ring in the harbor] *G;* Ent'ring into the harbor *D2;* Ent'ring the harbor *D1, A, H, C.*
24. What . . . her?] *G, D1, D2–C;* What became of those on board? *A.*
29–50.] *C omits through* I understand no riddles.
30. Here in Cornwall] *G, D1, D2, H;* In Cornwall here *A; om. C.*
31. Guiana] *G, D1, D2, H;* Guinea *A; om. C.*

30–36. *The brave . . . Spaniards*] Shortly after his return from an unsuccessful search for gold in Guiana, Ralegh was arrested near Plymouth by Sir Lewis Stukeley upon orders issued by James I at the insistence of Gondomar, the Spanish ambassador. Although Stukeley, Ralegh's cousin, acted in his official capacity as vice-admiral of Devonshire, he incurred lasting popular hatred and was called "Sir Judas Stukeley."

38–40. *There's . . . submit to*] Powerful Court and City factions felt that Spain's *insolence* was forcing the *pacific reign* of George II and Walpole toward open hostilities. As early as 1731 Lillo had shown himself sympathetic with these groups, and he here uses anti-Spanish material fortuitously suggested by his sources.

Poor England must submit to. Gallant man! 40
Posterity perhaps may do thee justice
And praise thy courage, learning, and integrity,
When thou'rt past hearing. Thy successful enemies,
Much sooner paid, have their reward in hand
And know for what they labor'd. Such events 45
Must, questionless, excite all thinking men
To love and practice virtue!

RANDAL. Nay, 'tis certain
That virtue ne'er appears so like itself,
So truly bright and great, as when oppress'd.

OLD WILMOT.
I understand no riddles. Where's your mistress? 50

RANDAL.
I saw her pass the High Street t'ward the minster.

OLD WILMOT.
She's gone to visit Charlot. [*Aside.*] She doth well.
In the soft bosom of that gentle maid
There dwells more goodness than the rigid race
Of moral pedants e'er believ'd or taught. 55
With what amazing constancy and truth
Doth she sustain the absence of our son
Whom more than life she loves! How shun for him,
Whom we shall ne'er see more, the rich and great,
Who own her charms more than supply the want 60
Of shining heaps, and sigh to make her happy!
Since our misfortunes, we have found no friend,
None who regarded our distress, but her.

40. submit to] *G, D1, D2, H;* submit t'it *A; om. C.*

60–61. more . . . heaps] *G–H; om. C.*

43–45. *Thy . . . labor'd*] Between the stories of Ralegh's betrayal and the Penryn murder, Sanderson and Frankland have a short item labeled "4 Earls created for mony": "Having paid the price, a good sum for their honours; so earnest some are, and so ambitious of preferment, as what they cannot get by merit, they covet to purchase with money." Old Wilmot, or Lillo, seems to connect this event with the Ralegh debacle.

51. *the High . . . minster*] Adolphus W. Ward points out that Lillo was not familiar with the Cornish setting of his play; the parish church of Penryn was never called a minster and was located a mile away from the High Street (*The London Merchant . . . and Fatal Curiosity* [Boston and London, 1906], p. xlviii).

And she, by what I have observed of late,
Is tired or exhausted. Curst condition! 65
To live a burden to one only friend,
And blast her youth with our contagious woe!
Who, that had reason, soul, or sense, would bear it
A moment longer?—Then, this honest wretch!—
I must dismiss him. Why should I detain 70
A grateful, gen'rous youth to perish with me?
His service may procure him bread elsewhere,
Though I have none to give him. —Prithee, Randal!
How long has thou been with me?

RANDAL. Fifteen years.
I was a very child when first you took me 75
To wait upon your son, my dear young master.
I oft have wished I'd gone to India with him,
Though you, desponding, give him o'er for lost.

Old Wilmot *wipes his eyes.*

I am to blame. This talk revives your sorrow
For his absence.

OLD WILMOT. How can that be reviv'd 80
Which never died?

RANDAL. The whole of my intent
Was to confess your bounty that supplied
The loss of both my parents. I was long
The object of your charitable care.

OLD WILMOT.
No more of that! Thou'st served me longer since 85
Without reward, so that account is balanced,
Or rather I'm thy debtor. I remember,
When poverty began to show her face
Within these walls, and all my other servants,
Like pamper'd vermin from a falling house, 90
Retreated with the plunder they had gained,
And left me, too indulgent and remiss
For such ungrateful wretches, to be crushed

65. tired or exhausted] *G, D1, D2, H;* tired or else exhausted *A;* wearied or exhausted *C.*

66. one only] *G, D1, D2–C;* one's only *A.*

92. too . . . remiss] *G, D1, D2–C;* too indulgent, too remiss *A.*

Beneath the ruin they had helped to make,
That you, more good than wise, refused to leave me— 95

RANDAL.
Nay, I beseech you, sir!

OLD WILMOT. —With my distresses.
In perfect contradiction to the world,
Thy love, respect, and diligence increased.
Now all the recompense within my power
Is to discharge thee, Randal, from my hard, 100
Unprofitable service.

RANDAL. Heaven forbid!
Shall I forsake you in your worst necessity?
Believe me, sir, my honest soul abhors
The barb'rous thought!

OLD WILMOT. What! Canst thou feed on air?
I have not left wherewith to purchase food 105
For one meal more.

RANDAL. Rather than leave you thus,
I'll beg my bread and live on others' bounty
While I serve you.

OLD WILMOT [*aside*]. Down, down, my swelling heart,
Or burst in silence! 'Tis thy cruel fate
Insults thee by his kindness. He is innocent 110
Of all the pain it gives thee. —Go thy ways!
I will no more suppress thy youthful hopes
Of rising in the world.

RANDAL. 'Tis true I'm young
And never tried my fortune or my genius,
Which may perhaps find out some happy means, 115
As yet unthought of, to supply your wants.

OLD WILMOT.
Thou tortur'st me! I hate all obligations
Which I can ne'er return. And who art thou
That I should stoop to take 'em from thy hand?
Care for thyself, but take no thought for me. 120
I will not want thee. Trouble me no more.

102. worst necessity] *G, D1, D2–C;* greatest need *A.*
106. For . . . more] *G, D1, D2–C;* For one month longer *A.*
113. I'm young] *G, D1, D2–C;* I am young *A.*

RANDAL.
Be not offended, sir, and I will go.
I ne'er repined at your commands before,
But, Heaven's my witness, I obey you now
With strong reluctance and a heavy heart. 125
Farewell, my worthy master! *Going.*

OLD WILMOT. Farewell. —Stay!
As thou art yet a stranger to the world,
Of which, alas, I've had too much experience,
I should, methinks, before we part, bestow
A little counsel on thee. Dry thy eyes. 130
If thou weep'st thus, I shall proceed no farther.
Dost thou aspire to greatness or to wealth,
Quit books and the unprofitable search
Of wisdom there, and study humankind.
No science will avail thee without that, 135
But, that obtained, thou need'st not any other.
This will instruct thee to conceal thy views
And wear the face of probity and honor
Till thou hast gained thy end, which must be ever
Thy own advantage at that man's expense 140
Who shall be weak enough to think thee honest.

RANDAL.
You mock me, sure!

OLD WILMOT. I never was more serious.

RANDAL.
Why should you counsel what you scorned to practice?

OLD WILMOT.
Because that foolish scorn has been my ruin.
I've been an idiot, but would have thee wiser 145
And treat mankind as they would treat thee, Randal,
As they deserve, and I've been treated by 'em.
Thou'st seen by me, and those who now despise me,
How men of fortune fall, and beggars rise.
Shun my example; treasure up my precepts. 150
The world's before thee. Be a knave, and prosper!
After a long pause.
What, art thou dumb?

132.] *C makes this line a question.*

RANDAL. Amazement ties my tongue.
Where are your former principles?

OLD WILMOT. No matter.
Suppose I have renounced 'em. I have passions
And love thee still; therefore, would have thee think 155
The world is all a scene of deep deceit,
And he who deals with mankind on the square
Is his own bubble and undoes himself. *Exit.*

RANDAL.
Is this the man I thought so wise and just?
What! Teach and counsel me to be a villain? 160
Sure, grief has made him frantic, or some fiend
Assumed his shape. I shall suspect my senses.
High-minded he was ever, and improvident,
But pitiful and generous to a fault.
Pleasure he loved, but honor was his idol. 165
Oh, fatal change! Oh, horrid transformation!
So a majestic temple sunk to ruin
Becomes the loathsome shelter and abode
Of lurking serpents, toads, and beasts of prey,
And scaly dragons hiss, and lions roar, 170
Where wisdom taught, and music charmed before. *Exit.*

[I.ii] *A parlor in Charlot's house.*
Enter Charlot *and* Maria.

CHARLOT.
What terror and amazement must they feel
Who die by shipwreck!

MARIA. 'Tis a dreadful thought.

CHARLOT.
Aye, is it not, Maria? To descend,
Living and conscious, to that wat'ry tomb.

158.] *C adds a line:* farewell, and mark my counsel, boy!

[I.ii]
1. they] *G, D1, D2–C;* those *A.*
4. that wat'ry] *G, A, D2;* the wat'ry *D1, H, C.*

---

158. *bubble*] dupe.

163. *high-minded*] In view of the balanced construction of ll. 163–164, the meaning is probably pejorative, indicating that Old Wilmot was proud *but* "pitiful," considerate of others.

Alas, had we no sorrows of our own, 5
The frequent instances of others' woes
Must give a gen'rous mind a world of pain.
But you forget you promised me to sing.
Though cheerfulness and I have long been strangers,
Harmonious sounds are still delightful to me. 10
There is in melody a secret charm
That flatters while it adds to my disquiet,
And makes the deepest sadness the most pleasing.
There's sure no passion in the human soul,
But finds its food in music. I would hear 15
The song composed by that unhappy maid
Whose faithful lover 'scaped a thousand perils
From rocks, and sand, and the devouring deep,
And, after all, being arrived at home,
Passing a narrow brook, was drowned there 20
And perished in her sight.

SONG

MARIA. *Cease, cease, heart-easing tears;*
Adieu, you flatt'ring fears,
Which seven long tedious years
Taught me to bear. 25
Tears are for lighter woes;
Fear no such danger knows
As Fate remorseless shows,
Endless despair.
Dear cause of all my pain, 30
On the wide stormy main
Thou wast preserved in vain,
Though still adored.
Had'st thou died there unseen,
My blasted eyes had been 35
Saved from the horrid'st scene
Maid e'er deplored.

Charlot *finds a letter.*

8–37.] *G, D1, D2–C; om. A.*
11–13.] *G, D1, D2, H; om. A, C.*
36. horrid'st] *G, D1, D2, H; om. A;* direst *C.*

CHARLOT.

What's this? A letter superscribed to me!
None could convey it here but you, Maria.
Ungen'rous, cruel maid! To use me thus, 40
To join with flatt'ring men to break my peace,
And persecute me to the last retreat!

MARIA.

Why should it break your peace to hear the sighs
Of honorable love and know th'effects
Of your resistless charms? This letter is— 45

CHARLOT.

No matter whence. Return it back unopened!
I have no love, no charms but for my Wilmot,
Nor would have any.

MARIA. Strange infatuation!
Why should you waste the flower of your days
In fruitless expectation? Wilmot's dead, 50
Or, living, dead to you.

CHARLOT. I'll not despair
(Patience shall cherish hope), nor wrong his honor
By unjust suspicion. I know his truth,
And will preserve my own. But to prevent
All future vain, officious importunity, 55
Know, thou incessant foe of my repose,
Whether he sleeps secure from mortal cares
In the deep bosom of the boist'rous main,
Or, tossed with tempests, still endures its rage;
Whether his weary pilgrimage by land 60
Has found an cnd and he now rests in peace
In earth's cold womb, or wanders o'er her face;
Be it my lot to waste, in pining grief,
The remnant of my days for his known loss
Or live, as now, uncertain and in doubt, 65
No second choice shall violate my vows.
High Heaven, which heard them and abhors the perjured,

44–45. and ... charms] *G–H; om. C.*
48–50. Strange ... expectation?] *G–H; om. C. In C Maria's speech begins:* Alas, Wilmot's dead.
54–56. But ... repose] *G–H; om. C.*
60–65.] *G–H, om. C.*

Can witness they were made without reserve,
Never to be retracted, ne'er dissolved
By accidents or absence, time or death! 70

MARIA.

I know, and long have known, my honest zeal
To serve you gives offense. But be offended!
This is no time for flatt'ry. Did your vows
Oblige you to support his gloomy, proud,
Impatient parents to your utter ruin? 75
You well may weep to think on what you've done.

CHARLOT.

I weep to think that I can do no more
For their support. What will become of 'em,
The hoary, helpless, miserable pair?

MARIA.

Then all these tears, this sorrow is for them? 80

CHARLOT.

Taught by afflictions, I have learned to bear
Much greater ills than poverty with patience.
When luxury and ostentation's banished,
The calls of nature are but few; and those,
These hands, not used to labor, may supply. 85
But when I think on what my friends must suffer,
My spirits fail, and I'm o'erwhelmed with grief.

MARIA.

What I would blame, you force me to admire
And mourn for you, as you lament for them.
Your patience, constancy, and resignation 90
Merit a better fate.

CHARLOT. So pride would tell me,

70. accidents] *G, A, D2;* accident *D1, H, C.*
71–73. I . . . flatt'ry] *G–H; om. C.*
73–75. Did . . . ruin?] *G–H;* And did your vows oblige you to support/ His haughty parents to your utter ruin? *C.*
76. You well may] *G–H;* Well you may *C.*
80–87.] *G–H; om. C.*
83. ostentation's] *G, D1, D2,* ostentation are *A.*
85. not used] *G, D1, D2, H;* unused *A.*
86. must] *G, D1, D2, H;* may *A.*
88. What . . . blame] *G–H;* What I can't praise *C.*
91. Merit] *G, D1, D2–C;* Deserves *A.*

And vain self-love, but I believe them not;
And if, by wanting pleasure, I have gained
Humility, I'm richer for my loss.

MARIA.
You have the heavenly art still to improve 95
Your mind by all events. —But here comes one
Whose pride seems to increase with her misfortunes.

Enter Agnes.

Her faded dress, unfashionably fine,
As ill conceals her poverty as that
Strained complaisance her haughty, swelling heart. 100
Though perishing with want, so far from asking,
She ne'er receives a favor uncompelled,
And, while she ruins, scorns to be obliged.
She wants me gone, and I abhor her sight. *Exit* Maria.

CHARLOT.
This visit's kind.

AGNES. Few else would think it so. 105
Those who would once have thought themselves much honored
By the least favor, though 'twere but a look
I could have shown them, now refuse to see me.
'Tis misery enough to be reduced
To the low level of the common herd 110
Who, born to begg'ry, envy all above them,
But 'tis the curse of curses to endure
The insolent contempt of those we scorn.

CHARLOT.
By scorning we provoke them to contempt,
And thus offend, and suffer in our turns. 115
We must have patience.

AGNES. No, I scorn them yet!
But there's no end of suff'ring. Who can say
Their sorrows are complete? My wretched husband,
Tired with our woes and hopeless of relief,
Grows sick of life.

94. for] *G, D1, D2–C;* by *A.*
104.] *G–H;* Let me depart. I know she loves me not. *C.*
105. S.P. AGNES] *G, D1, D2–C;* Lady Wilmot *A.*

CHARLOT. May gracious Heaven support him! 120

AGNES.
And, urged by indignation and despair,
Would plunge into eternity at once
By foul self-murder. His fixed love for me,
Whom he would fain persuade to share his fate
And take the same, uncertain, dreadful course, 125
Alone withholds his hand.

CHARLOT. And may it ever!

AGNES.
I've known with him the two extremes of life,
The highest happiness and deepest woe,
With all the sharp and bitter aggravations
Of such a vast transition. Such a fall 130
In the decline of life! I have as quick,
As exquisite a sense of pain as he,
And would do anything, but die, to end it.
But there my courage fails. Death is the worst
That fate can bring, and cuts off ev'ry hope. 135

CHARLOT.
We must not choose, but strive to bear our lot
Without reproach or guilt. But by one act
Of desperation we may overthrow
The merit we've been raising all our days,
And lose our whole reward. And now, methinks, 140
Now more than ever, we have cause to fear
And be upon our guard. The hand of Heaven
Spreads clouds on clouds o'er our benighted heads
And, wrapped in darkness, doubles our distress.
I had the night last past, repeated twice, 145
A strange and awful dream. I would not yield
To fearful superstition, nor despise
The admonition of a friendly power
That wished my good.

AGNES. I've certain plagues enough,

120–123.] *C transfers Charlot's exclamation to l. 123 (after* self-murder) *and changes it to* Gracious Heav'n support him!

121. And, urged] *G, D1, D2–C;* He, urged *A.*

137. But . . . act] *G, A, D2;* By one rash act *D1, H, C.*

Without the help of dreams, to make me wretched. 150

CHARLOT.

I would not stake my happiness or duty
On their uncertain credit, nor on aught
But reason and the known decrees of Heaven.
Yet, dreams have sometimes shown events to come,
And may excite to vigilance and care 155
In some important hour when all our weakness
Shall be attacked and all our strength be needed
To shun the gulf that gapes for our destruction,
And fly from guilt and everlasting ruin.
My vision may be such, and sent to warn us, 160
Now we are tried by multiplied afflictions,
To mark each motion of our swelling hearts
And not attempt to extricate ourselves
And seek deliverance by forbidden ways,
But keep our hopes and innocence entire 165
Till we're dismissed to join the happy dead
In that bless'd world where transitory pain
And frail imperfect virtue is rewarded
With endless pleasure and consummate joy,
Or Heaven relieves us here.

AGNES. Well, pray proceed. 170

You've raised my curiosity at least.

CHARLOT.

Methought I sat, in a dark winter's night,
My garments thin, my head and bosom bare,
On the wide summit of a barren mountain,
Defenseless and exposed in that high region 175
To all the cruel rigors of the season.
The sharp, bleak winds pierced through my shiv'ring frame,
And storms of hail and sleet and driving rains
Beat with impetuous fury on my head,
Drenched my chilled limbs, and poured a deluge round me. 180
On one hand ever-gentle Patience sat,
On whose calm bosom I reclined my head,

156–159.] *G–H; om. C.*
165. But keep] *G, A, D2;* To keep *D1, H, C.*
173.] *G–H; om. C.*
175–176.] *G–H; om. C.*
182. reclined] *G–A, H, C;* declined *D2.*

And on the other, silent Contemplation.
At length to my unclosed and watchful eyes,
That long had rolled in darkness and oft raised 185
Their cheerless orbs towards the starless sky
And sought for light in vain, the dawn appeared.
And I beheld a man, an utter stranger
But of a graceful and exalted mien,
Who pressed with eager transport to embrace me. 190
I shunned his arms, but at some words he spoke,
Which I have now forgot, I turned again,
But he was gone, and, oh, transporting sight!
Your son, my dearest Wilmot, filled his place!

AGNES.
If I regarded dreams, I should expect 195
Some fair event from yours. I have heard nothing
That should alarm you yet.

CHARLOT. But what's to come,
Though more obscure, is terrible indeed.
Methought we parted soon and, when I sought him,
You and his father—yes, you both were there— 200
Strove to conceal him from me. I pursued
You with my cries, and called on Heaven and earth
To judge my wrongs and force you to reveal
Where you had hid my love, my life, my Wilmot!

AGNES.
Unless you mean t'affront me, spare the rest. 205
'Tis just as likely Wilmot should return
As we become your foes.

CHARLOT. Far be such rudeness
From Charlot's thoughts. But when I heard you name
Self-murder, it revived the frightful image
Of such a dreadful scene.

AGNES. You will persist! 210

185–187. and . . . vain] *G–H; om. C.*
196–197. I . . . yet] *G–H; om. C.*
200. you both] *G, D1, D2–C;* ye both *A.*
201–202. pursued/ You with] *G–H;* pursued you/ Both with *C.*
205. affront] *G–H;* offend *C.*
207. rudeness] *G–H;* thought *C.*
208. thoughts] *G–H;* breast *C.*
208. Charlot's . . . name] *G, D1, D2, H;* Charlotta's thoughts,/ But when you named *A;* For be such thought/ From Charlot's breast . . . name *C.*

CHARLOT.

Excuse me. I have done. Being a dream,
I thought, indeed, it could not give offense.

AGNES.

Not when the matter of it is offensive?
You could not think so, had you thought at all.
But I take nothing ill from thee. Adieu, 215
I've tarried longer than I first intended,
And my poor husband mourns the while alone. *Exit* Agnes.

CHARLOT.

She's gone abruptly and, I fear, displeased.
The least appearance of advice or caution
Sets her impatient temper in a flame. 220
When grief, that well might humble, swells our pride,
And pride, increasing, aggravates our grief,
The tempest must prevail till we are lost.
When Heaven, incensed, proclaims unequal war
With guilty earth and sends its shafts from far, 225
No bolt descends to strike, no flame to burn,
The humble shrubs that in low valleys mourn;
While mountain pines, whose lofty heads aspire
To fan the storm and wave in fields of fire,
And stubborn oaks, that yield not to its force, 230
Are burnt, o'erthrown, or shivered in its course.
[*Exit* Charlot.]

[I.iii] *The town and port of Penryn.*
Enter Young Wilmot *and* Eustace *in Indian habits.*

YOUNG WILMOT.

Welcome, my friend, to Penryn! Here we're safe.

211. Being] *G, D1, D2–C;* As 'twas *A.*
212. indeed] *G–H;* at least *C.*
213.] *G–H; om. C.*
224–231.] *G–H; om. C. Instead, Charlot says:* Heaven grant a fairer issue to her sorrows.
[I.iii]
0.2. *Indian*] *G–A, H, C;* India *D2.*

0.1. *in . . . habits*] This costume is not improbable for the period. Contemporary newspapers commented on the attire of English prisoners rescued from Barbary captivity; Defoe has Captain Singleton and his friend return to England disguised in the "long Vests" of Persian-Armenian-Grecian merchants.

EUSTACE.
Then we're delivered twice: first, from the sea,
And then from savage men who, more remorseless,
Prey on shipwrecked wretches and spoil and murder those
Whom fatal tempests and devouring waves, 5
In all their fury, spared.

YOUNG WILMOT. It is a scandal
(Though malice must acquit the better sort)
The rude, unpolished people here in Cornwall
Have long laid under, and with too much justice.
Could our superiors find some happy means 10
To mend it, they would gain immortal honor,
For 'tis an evil grown almost invet'rate,
And asks a bold and skilful hand to cure.

EUSTACE.
Your treasure's safe, I hope.

YOUNG WILMOT. 'Tis here, thank Heaven!
Being in jewels, when I saw our danger, 15
I hid it in my bosom.

EUSTACE. I observed you,
And wonder how you could command your thoughts
In such a time of terror and confusion.

YOUNG WILMOT.
My thoughts were then at home. Oh, England, England!
Thou seat of plenty, liberty, and health! 20
With transport I behold thy verdant fields,
Thy lofty mountains rich with useful ore,
Thy numerous herds, thy flocks, and winding streams!
After a long and tedious absence, Eustace,
With what delight we breathe our native air 25

3. savage] *G, D2, A; om. D1, H, C.*
4. and spoil and murder] *G, D2;* and who spoil and murder *D1, H, C;* murd'ring *A.*
5. fatal] *G–H;* fell *C.*
10–11.] *G–H; om. C.*
17. wonder] *G–A, H, C;* wonder'd *D2.*

2–13. *Then . . . cure*] In *The London Merchant* (IV.xviii) Millwood denounces "suburb-magistrates, who live by ruined reputations, as the inhospitable natives of Cornwall do by shipwrecks." Here the Cornish setting and the allusion to plundering serve an ironic purpose. It is *the better sort*, such as the elder Wilmots, who prove to be the savage and remorseless pillagers.

And tread the genial soil that bore us first.
'Tis said the world is ev'ry wise man's country;
Yet, after having viewed its various nations,
I'm weak enough still to prefer my own
To all I've seen beside. You smile, my friend, 30
And think, perhaps, 'tis instinct more than reason.
Why, be it so! Instinct preceded reason
In the wisest of us all, and may sometimes
Be much the better guide. But be it either,
I must confess that even death itself 35
Appeared to me with twice its native horrors
When apprehended in a foreign land.
Death is, no doubt, in ev'ry place the same;
Yet observation must convince us most men,
Who have it in their power, choose to expire 40
Where they first drew their breath.

EUSTACE. Believe me, Wilmot,
Your grave reflections were not what I smiled at.
I own their truth. That we're returned to England
Affords me all the pleasure you can feel
Merely on that account. Yet I must think 45
A warmer passion gives you all this transport.
You have not wandered, anxious and impatient,
From clime to clime, and compassed sea and land
To purchase wealth, only to spend your days
In idle pomp and luxury at home. 50
I know thee better; thou art brave and wise,
And must have nobler aims.

YOUNG WILMOT. Oh, Eustace, Eustace!
Thou knowest, for I've confessed to thee, I love.
But, having never seen the charming maid,
Thou canst not know the fierceness of my flame. 55
My hopes and fears, like the tempestuous seas
That we have passed, now mount me to the skies,
Now hurl me down from that stupendous height

39.] *G, A, D2;* Yet observation must convince us, most *D1, H;* Yet nature casts a look towards home and most *C.*
44. their] *G–H;* the *C.*
45–52. Yet . . . aims] *G–H; om. C, which substitutes:* Yet I must think a warmer passion moves you:/ Thinking of that I smiled.

And drive me to the center. Did you know
How much depends on this important hour, 60
You would not be surprised to see me thus.
The sinking fortune of our ancient house,
Which time and various accidents had wasted,
Compelled me young to leave my native country,
My weeping parents, and my lovely Charlot, 65
Who ruled and must forever rule my fate.
How I've improved, by care and honest commerce,
My little stock, you are in part a witness.
'Tis now seven tedious years since I set forth
And, as th'uncertain course of my affairs 70
Bore me from place to place, I quickly lost
The means of corresponding with my friends.
Oh, should my Charlot, doubtful of my truth
Or in despair ever to see me more,
Have given herself to some more happy lover! 75
Distraction's in the thought! Or should my parents,
Grieved for my absence and oppressed with want,
Have sunk beneath their burden and expired,
While I, too late, was flying to relieve them,
The end of all my long and weary travels, 80
The hope, that made success itself a blessing,
Being defeated and forever lost,
What were the riches of the world to me?

EUSTACE.
The wretch who fears all that is possible
Must suffer more than he who feels the worst 85
A man can feel who lives exempt from fear.
A woman may be false, and friends are mortal.
And yet your aged parents may be living,
And your fair mistress constant.

YOUNG WILMOT. True, they may.
I doubt, but I despair not. No, my friend, 90
My hopes are strong and lively as my fears,
And give me such a prospect of my happiness
As nothing but fruition can exceed.

63.] *G–H; om. C.*
67–72.] *G–H; om. C.*
86. who] *G, A, D2;* yet *D1, H, C.*
92–93.] *G–H; om. C.*

They tell me Charlot is as true as fair,
As good as wise, as passionate as chaste; 95
That she, with fierce impatience like my own,
Laments our long and painful separation;
That we shall meet, never to part again;
That I shall see my parents, kiss the tears
From their pale hollow cheeks, cheer their sad hearts, 100
And drive that gaping phantom, meager Want,
Forever from their board, crown all their days
To come with peace, with pleasure, and abundance,
Receive their fond embraces and their blessings,
And be a blessing to 'em.

EUSTACE. 'Tis our weakness: 105
Blind to events, we reason in the dark,
And fondly apprehend what none e'er found
Or ever shall: pleasure and pain unmixed;
And flatter, and torment ourselves, by turns
With what shall never be.

YOUNG WILMOT. I'll go this instant 110
To seek my Charlot and explore my fate.

EUSTACE.
What! In that foreign habit?

YOUNG WILMOT. That's a trifle
Not worth my thoughts.

EUSTACE. The hardships you've endured
And your long stay beneath the burning zone,
Where one eternal sultry summer reigns, 115
Have marred the native hue of your complexion.
Methinks you look more like a sun-burnt Indian
Than a Briton.

YOUNG WILMOT. Well, 'tis no matter, Eustace!
I hope my mind's not altered for the worse,
And for my outside— But inform me, friend, 120
When I may hope to see you.

EUSTACE. When you please.
You'll find me at the inn.

95–97.] *G–H; om. C.*
102–103. crown . . . peace] *G, A, D2;* their days to come/ Crown all with peace. *D1, H, C.*

120. *And for*] And, as for.
122.] This is the first break in Lillo's blank verse.

YOUNG WILMOT.

When I have learnt my doom, expect me there.
Till then, farewell!

EUSTACE. Farewell! Success attend you! *Exit* Eustace.

YOUNG WILMOT.

"We flatter, and torment ourselves, by turns, 125
With what shall never be." Amazing folly!
We stand exposed to many unavoidable
Calamities and therefore fondly labor
T'increase their number and enforce their weight
By our fantastic hopes and groundless fears. 130

For one severe distress imposed by Fate,
What numbers doth tormenting Fear create,
Deceived by hope, Ixion-like, we prove
Immortal joys and seem to rival Jove.
The cloud dissolved, impatient we complain, 135
And pay for fancied bliss substantial pain.

[*Exit* Young Wilmot.]

124.1] *G, D1, D2, H; om. A;* (*Exeunt severally.*) *C.* 125–136.] *G–H; om. C.*

---

133. *Ixion-like*] In Greek mythology, Ixion was carried to Heaven by Zeus, where he became enamoured of Hera and boasted that he had seduced her. As punishment he was banished to Hell and tied to a perpetually revolving wheel.

ACT II

[II.i] *Charlot's house.*

Enter Charlot, *thoughtful; and, soon after,* Maria, *from the other side.*

MARIA.

Madam, a stranger in a foreign habit
Desires to see you.

CHARLOT. In a foreign habit?
'Tis strange and unexpected, but admit him. *Exit* Maria.
What can this stranger be? I know no foreigner.

Enter Young Wilmot.

Nor any man like this.

YOUNG WILMOT. Ten thousand joys! *Going to embrace her.* 5

CHARLOT.

You are rude, sir. Pray forbear and let me know
What business brought you here, or leave the place.

YOUNG WILMOT (*aside*).

She knows me not, or will not seem to know me.—
Perfidious maid! Am I forgot, or scorned?

CHARLOT.

Strange questions from a man I never knew! 10

YOUNG WILMOT (*aside*).

With what aversion and contempt she views me!
My fears are true; some other has her heart.
She's lost! My fatal absence has undone me!—
Oh, could thy Wilmot have forgot thee, Charlot!

CHARLOT.

Ha! Wilmot! Say, what do your words import? 15
Oh, gentle stranger, ease my swelling heart
That else will burst! Canst thou inform me aught?
What dost thou know of Wilmot?

YOUNG WILMOT. This I know:

0.2. *soon after,* Maria] *G, D1, D2, H; and her maid* Maria *A; soon after a servant C.*
3.1.] *G, D1, D2, H; om. A; (Exit Servant.) C.*
6. You . . . forbear] *G–H;* Sir, you are too too bold. Forbear. *C.*
8.] *G–H; om. C.*
17.] *G–H; om. C.*
18. of Wilmot] *G, D1, D2–C;* of my Wilmot *A.*

When all the winds of heaven seemed to conspire
Against the stormy main, and dreadful peals 20
Of rattling thunder deafened ev'ry ear
And drowned th'affrightened mariners' loud cries;
While livid lightning spread its sulphurous flames
Through all the dark horizon and disclosed
The raging seas incensed to his destruction; 25
When the good ship in which he was embarked,
Unable longer to support the tempest,
Broke and, o'erwhelmed by the impetuous surge,
Sunk to the oozy bottom of the deep
And left him struggling with the warring waves— 30
In that dread moment, in the jaws of death,
When his strength failed, and ev'ry hope forsook him,
And his last breath pressed t'wards his trembling lips,
The neighboring rocks, that echoed to his moan,
Returned no sound articulate but "Charlot." 35

CHARLOT.

The fatal tempest, whose description strikes
The hearer with astonishment, is ceased,
And Wilmot is at rest. The fiercer storm
Of swelling passions that o'erwhelms the soul
And rages worse than the mad foaming seas 40
In which he perished, ne'er shall vex him more.

YOUNG WILMOT.

Thou seem'st to think he's dead. Enjoy that thought!
Persuade yourself that what you wish is true,
And triumph in your falsehood! Yes, he's dead.
You were his fate. The cruel winds and waves 45
That cast him pale and breathless on the shore
Spared him for greater woes—to know his Charlot,
Forgetting all her vows to him and Heaven,
Had cast him from her thoughts. Then, then he died,
But never must have rest. Ev'n now he wanders, 50
A sad, repining, discontented ghost,
The unsubstantial shadow of himself,

23. While] *G, A, D2;* When *D1, H, C.*
27.] *G–H; om. C.*
50. never must] *G, A, D2;* never can *D1, H, C.*

And pours his plaintive groans in thy deaf ears,
And stalks, unseen, before thee.

CHARLOT. 'Tis enough!
Detested falsehood now has done its worst. 55
And art thou dead? And would'st thou die, my Wilmot,
For one thou thought'st unjust? Thou soul of truth!
What must be done? Which way shall I express
Unutterable woe? Or how convince
Thy dear, departed spirit of the love, 60
Th'eternal love, and never-failing faith
Of thy much-injured, lost, despairing Charlot?

YOUNG WILMOT [*aside*].
Be still, my flutt'ring heart; hope not too soon.
Perhaps I dream, and this is all illusion.

CHARLOT.
If, as some teach, the mind intuitive, 65
Free from the narrow bounds and slavish ties
Of sordid earth that circumscribe its power
While it remains below, roving at large,
Can trace us to our most concealed retreat,
See all we act, and read our very thoughts, 70
To thee, O Wilmot, kneeling I appeal!
If e'er I swerved in action, word, or thought
From the severest constancy and truth,
Or ever wished to taste a joy on earth
That centered not in thee, since last we parted, 75
May we ne'er meet again but thy loud wrongs
So close the ear of Mercy to my cries
That I may never see those bright abodes
Where truth and virtue only have admission,
And thou inhabit'st now.

YOUNG WILMOT [*aside*]. Assist me, Heaven! 80
Preserve my reason, memory, and sense!
Oh, moderate my fierce tumultuous joys,

58–59.] *G, D1, D2–C;* Oh, how shall I convince *A.*
65. the mind intuitive] *G–H;* the spirit after death *C.*
66–68. the . . . large] *G–H;* the bounds and ties of sordid earth *C.*
73. and truth] *G–A, H;* of truth *D2; om. C.*
79. admission] *G, D1, D2–C;* access *A.*

Or their excess will drive me to distraction.—
Oh, Charlot, Charlot! Lovely, virtuous maid!
Can thy firm mind, in spite of time and absence, 85
Remain unshaken and support its truth,
And yet thy frailer memory retain
No image, no idea of thy lover?
Why dost thou gaze so wildly? Look on me;
Turn thy dear eyes this way; observe me well. 90
Have scorching climates, time, and this strange habit
So changed and so disguised thy faithful Wilmot
That nothing in my voice, my face, or mien,
Remains to tell my Charlot I am he?

After viewing him some time, she approaches weeping and gives him her hand, and then, turning towards him, sinks upon his bosom.

Why dost thou weep? Why dost thou tremble thus? 95
Why doth thy panting heart and cautious touch
Speak thee but half-convinced? Whence are thy fears?
Why art thou silent? Canst thou doubt me still?

CHARLOT.
No, Wilmot, no! I'm blind with too much light,
O'ercome with wonder, and oppressed with joy. 100
The struggling passions barred the doors of speech,
But speech, enlarged, affords me no relief.
This vast profusion of extreme delight,
Rising at once and bursting from despair,
Defies the aid of words and mocks description. 105
But for one sorrow, one sad scene of anguish
That checks the swelling torrent of my joys,
I could not bear the transport.

YOUNG WILMOT. Let me know it.
Give me my portion of thy sorrow, Charlot.
Let me partake thy grief, or bear it for thee. 110

CHARLOT.
Alas, my Wilmot, these sad tears are thine!
They flow for thy misfortunes. I am pierced
With all the agonies of strong compassion,

94.1–2.] *A changes the verbs to past tense.* 101–102.] *G–H; om. C.*

With all the bitter anguish you must feel,
When you shall hear your parents—

YOUNG WILMOT. Are no more. 115

CHARLOT.
You apprehend me wrong.

YOUNG WILMOT. Perhaps I do.
Perhaps you mean to say, the greedy grave
Was satisfied with one, and one is left
To bless my longing eyes. But which, my Charlot,
And yet, forbear to speak, till I have thought— 120

CHARLOT.
Nay, hear me, Wilmot!

YOUNG WILMOT. I, perforce, must hear thee,
For I might think till death and not determine
Of two so dear which I could bear to lose.

CHARLOT.
Afflict yourself no more with groundless fears.
Your parents both are living. Their distress, 125
The poverty to which they are reduced,
In spite of my weak aid, was what I mourned,
And that, in helpless age, to them whose youth
Was crowned with full prosperity, I fear,
Is worse, much worse, than death.

YOUNG WILMOT. My joy's complete! 130
My parents living, and possessed of thee!
From this blest hour, the happiest of my life,
I'll date my rest. My anxious hopes and fears,
My weary travels, and my dangers past,
Are now rewarded all. Now I rejoice 135
In my success and count my riches gain,
For, know, my soul's best treasure, I have wealth
Enough to glut ev'n Avarice itself!
No more shall cruel want, or proud contempt,
Oppress the sinking spirits, or insult 140
The hoary heads of those who gave me being.

CHARLOT.
'Tis now, O riches, I conceive your worth!

121–123.] *G–H; om. C.*

128. And . . . age] *G–H;* That poverty in age *C.*

You are not base, nor can you be superfluous
But when misplaced in base and sordid hands.
Fly, fly, my Wilmot! Leave thy happy Charlot! 145
Thy filial piety, the sighs and tears
Of thy lamenting parents call thee hence.

YOUNG WILMOT.
I have a friend, the partner of my voyage,
Who in the storm last night was shipwrecked with me.

CHARLOT.
Shipwrecked last night? O you immortal Powers! 150
What have you suffered? How was you preserved?

YOUNG WILMOT.
Let that, and all my other strange escapes
And perilous adventures, be the theme
Of many a happy winter night to come.
My present purpose was t'entreat my angel 155
To know this friend, this other, better Wilmot
And come with him this evening to my father's.
I'll send him to thee.

CHARLOT. I consent with pleasure.

YOUNG WILMOT.
Heavens! What a night! How shall I bear my joy?
My parents', yours, my friend's, all will be mine, 160
And mine, like water, air, or the free splendid sun,
The undivided portion of you all.
If such the early hopes, the vernal bloom,
The distant prospect of my future bliss,
Then what the ruddy autumn! What the fruit! 165
The full possession of thy heavenly charms!
The tedious, dark, and stormy winter o'er,
The hind, that all its pinching hardships bore,
With transport sees the weeks appointed bring
The cheerful, promised, gay, delightful spring. 170
The painted meadows, the harmonious woods,
The gentle zephyrs, and unbridled floods,

151. was] *G, D1, D2, H;* were *A, C.*
161. splendid] *G, D1, D2, H; om. A.*
161–162.] *G–H; om. C.*
167–174.] *G–H; om. C.*

---

168. *hind*] farm laborer, rustic.

With all their charms, his ravished thoughts employ,
But the rich harvest must complete his joy.

[*Exeunt severally.*]

[II.ii] *A street in Penryn.*
Enter Randal.

RANDAL.

Poor! poor! and friendless! Whither shall I wander?
And to what point direct my views and hopes?
A menial servant? No! What, shall I live
Here in this land of freedom, live distinguished
And marked the willing slave of some proud subject 5
And swell his useless train for broken fragments,
The cold remains of his superfluous board?
I would aspire to something more and better.
Turn thy eyes then to the prolific ocean
Whose spacious bosom opens to thy view. 10
There deathless honor and unenvied wealth
Have often crowned the brave adventurer's toils.
This is the native uncontested right,
The fair inheritance of ev'ry Briton
That dares put in his claim. My choice is made. 15
A long farewell to Cornwall, and to England!
If I return—but stay, what stranger's this,
Who, as he views me, seems to mend his pace?

Enter Young Wilmot.

YOUNG WILMOT.

Randal! The dear companion of my youth!
Sure, lavish fortune means to give me all 20
I could desire, or ask for, this blest day
And leave me nothing to expect hereafter.

RANDAL.

Your pardon, sir. I know but one on earth
Could properly salute me by the title
You're pleased to give me, and I would not think 25
That you are he, that you are Wilmot.

6. And] *G, A, D2;* To *D1, H, C.*
8. more and better] *G, D1, D2–C;* nobler far *A.*
11. There] *G, D1, D2–C;* Where *A.*

YOUNG WILMOT. Why?

RANDAL.
Because I could not bear the disappointment
Should I be deceived.

YOUNG WILMOT. I am pleased to hear it.
Thy friendly fears better express thy thoughts
Than words could do.

RANDAL. Oh, Wilmot! Oh, my master! 30
Are you returned?

YOUNG WILMOT. I have not yet embraced
My parents. I shall see you at my father's.

RANDAL.
No, I'm discharged from thence. Oh, sir, such ruin—

YOUNG WILMOT.
I've heard it all, and hasten to relieve 'em.
Sure, Heaven hath blessed me to that very end. 35
I've wealth enough, nor shalt thou want a part.

RANDAL.
I have a part already. I am blest
In your success, and share in all your joys.

YOUNG WILMOT.
I doubt it not. But tell me, dost thou think,
My parents not suspecting my return, 40
That I may visit them and not be known?

RANDAL.
'Tis hard to judge. You are already
Grown so familiar to me that I wonder
I knew you not at first. Yet it may be,
For you're much altered, and they think you dead. 45

YOUNG WILMOT.
This is certain: Charlot beheld me long
And heard my loud reproaches and complaints
Without rememb'ring she had ever seen me.
My mind at ease grows wanton. I would fain
Refine on happiness. Why may I not 50
Indulge my curiosity, and try,
If it be possible, by seeing first

28. Should I be] *G, D1, D2, H;*
If I should be *A, C.*

My parents as a stranger, to improve
Their pleasure by surprise?

RANDAL. It may, indeed,
Enhance your own to see from what despair 55
Your timely coming and unhoped success
Have given you power to raise them.

YOUNG WILMOT. I remember
E'er since we learned together, you excelled
In writing fairly and could imitate
Whatever hand you saw with great exactness. 60
Of this I'm not so absolute a master.
I therefore beg you'll write, in Charlot's name
And character, a letter to my father
And recommend me, as a friend of hers,
To his acquaintance.

RANDAL. Sir, if you desire it— 65
And yet—

YOUNG WILMOT. Nay, no objections! 'Twill save time,
Most precious with me now. For the deception,
If doing what my Charlot will approve
'Cause done for me and with a good intent
Deserves the name, I'll answer it myself. 70
If this succeeds, I purpose to defer
Discovering who I am till Charlot comes,
And thou, and all who love me. Ev'ry friend
Who witnesses my happiness tonight
Will, by partaking, multiply my joys! 75

RANDAL.
You grow luxurious in your mental pleasures.
Could I deny you aught, I would not write
This letter. To say true, I ever thought
Your boundless curiosity a weakness.

YOUNG WILMOT.
What canst thou blame in this?

RANDAL. Your pardon, sir. 80

62.] *G–H; om. C.*
66. objections] *G, D1, D2–C;* objection *A.*
76. in ... pleasures] *G–H;* in imagination *C.*

67. *For*] As for.

I only speak in general. I'm ready
T'obey your orders.

YOUNG WILMOT. I am much thy debtor,
But I shall find a time to quit thy kindness.
Oh, Randal, but imagine to thyself
The floods of transport, the sincere delight 85
That all my friends will feel when I disclose
To my astonished parents my return,
And then confess that I have well contrived,
By giving others joy, t'exalt my own.
As pain and anguish, in a gen'rous mind, 90
While kept concealed and to ourselves confined,
Want half their force, so pleasure, when it flows
In torrents round us, more ecstatic grows. *Exeunt.*

[II.iii] *A room in Old Wilmot's house.*
Old Wilmot *and* Agnes.

OLD WILMOT.
Here, take this Seneca, this haughty pedant,
Who, governing the master of mankind
And awing power imperial, prates of patience!
And praises poverty, possessed of millions.
Sell him, and buy us bread. The scantiest meal 5
The vilest copy of his book e'er purchased

81. I . . . general] *G–H;* Perhaps I spoke too freely *C.*
90–93.] *G H; om. C.*

83. *quit*] requite, repay.

[II.iii]

1. *Here . . . Seneca*] The "Discovered, reading" scene was a dramatic commonplace. This one, however, may echo Addison's *Cato*, in which the hero is discovered reading Plato and debating the morality of suicide. Presumably Old Wilmot would be reading L'Estrange's translation of Seneca's *Morals of a Happy Life*, first published in 1693. Part II, Chapter XXV, entitled "Poverty, to a Wise Man, is rather a Blessing than a Misfortune," includes the following statements: "Shall I call him Poor that wants nothing, though he may be beholden for it to his Patience, rather than to his Fortune," and "Bread, when a Man is hungry, does his Work, be it never so coarse." The sale catalogue of Lillo's iibrary lists "Seneca's Morals. 1720."

2. *master . . . mankind*] Nero.

4. *millions*] Seneca reputedly possessed three hundred million sesterces.

Will give us more relief in this distress
Than all his boasted precepts. Nay, no tears!
Keep them to move compassion when you beg.

AGNES.
My heart may break, but never stoop to that. 10

OLD WILMOT.
Nor would I live to see it. But dispatch! *Exit* Agnes.
Where must I charge this length of misery
That gathers force each moment as it rolls
And must at last o'erwhelm me, but on hope,
Vain, flattering, delusive, groundless hope, 15
A senseless expectation of relief
That has for years deceived me? Had I thought
As I do now, as wise men ever think,
When first this hell of poverty o'ertook me,
That power to die implies a right to do it 20
And should be used when life becomes a pain,
What plagues had I prevented? True, my wife
Is still a slave to prejudice and fear.
I would not leave my better part, the dear, *Weeps.*
Faithful companion of my happier days, 25
To bear the weight of age and want alone.
I'll try once more.

Enter Agnes *and, after her,* Young Wilmot.

Returned, my life, so soon?

AGNES.
The unexpected coming of this stranger
Prevents my going yet.

YOUNG WILMOT. You're, I presume,
The gentleman to whom this is directed. *Gives a letter.* 30
[*Aside.*] What wild neglect, the token of despair,
What indigence, what misery appears
In each disordered or disfurnished room
Of this once gorgeous house! What discontent,

16.] *G–H; om. C.*
27. I'll . . . more] *G, D1, D2–C; om. A.*
33–34. In . . . house!] *G, D1, D2, H;* In . . . hall! *A;* In this once happy house! *C.*

12. *charge*] fix the blame for.

What anguish and confusion fill the faces 35
Of its dejected owners!

OLD WILMOT. Sir, such welcome
As this poor house affords, you may command.
Our ever-friendly neighbor—once we hoped
T'have called fair Charlot by a dearer name;
But we have done with hope—I pray, excuse 40
This incoherence. We had once a son. *Weeps.*

AGNES.
That you are come from that dear virtuous maid
Revives in us the mem'ry of a loss
Which, though long since, we have not learned to bear.

YOUNG WILMOT (*aside*).
The joy to see them, and the bitter pain 45
It is to see them thus, touches my soul
With tenderness and grief that will o'erflow.
My bosom heaves and swells as it would burst,
My bowels move, and my heart melts within me.
They know me not, and yet I fear I shall 50
Defeat my purpose and betray myself.

OLD WILMOT.
The lady calls you here her valued friend.
Enough, though nothing more should be implied,
To recommend you to our best esteem—
A worthless acquisition! May she find 55
Some means that better may express her kindness.
But she, perhaps, hath purposed to enrich
You with herself and end her fruitless sorrow
For one whom death alone can justify
For leaving her so long. If it be so, 60
May you repair his loss and be to Charlot

36.] *G, D1, D2–C; see Appendix A for lines added in A.*
40–41.] *G, D1, D2–C;* But we have done with hope. We'd once a son. (*Weeps.*)/ Excuse this incoherence. *A.*
48–49.] *G, D1, D2, H; om. C; A om. l. 49.*
53. implied] *G, D1, D2–C;* employed *A.*

49. *bowels*] tender feelings or pity, in the Biblical sense. See, in the King James Version, Phil. 2:1, "bowels and mercies"; Col. 3:12, "bowels of mercies"; I John 3:17, "bowels of compassion." The phrase *my heart melts* in this context also has Biblical overtones.

A second, happier Wilmot. Partial Nature,
Who only favors youth (as feeble age
Were not her offspring, or below her care),
Has sealed our doom. No second hope shall spring 65
From my dead loins and Agnes' sterile womb
To dry our tears and dissipate despair.

AGNES.
The last and most abandoned of our kind,
By Heaven and earth neglected or despised,
The loathsome grave, that robbed us of our son 70
And all our joys in him, must be our refuge.

YOUNG WILMOT.
Let ghosts unpardoned, or devoted fiends,
Fear without hope, and wail in such sad strains;
But grace defend the living from despair.
The darkest hours precede the rising sun, 75
And mercy may appear when least expected.

OLD WILMOT.
This I have heard a thousand times repeated,
And have, believing, been as oft deceived.

YOUNG WILMOT.
Behold in me an instance of its truth.
At sea twice shipwrecked, and as oft the prey 80
Of lawless pirates; by the Arabs thrice
Surprised and robbed on shore; and once reduced
To worse than these, the sum of all distress
That the most wretched feel on this side Hell—
Ev'n slavery itself. Yet here I stand, 85
Except one trouble that will quickly end,
The happiest of mankind.

66.] *G, D1, D2, H; om. A, C.* 82. once] *D1–C;* one *G.*

---

63. *as*] as if.
72. *devoted*] doomed.
79–85. *Behold . . . itself*] In the Sanderson and Frankland accounts, the son's ship explodes in "the Straits" (of Gibraltar), and he is later shipwrecked on the coast of Cornwall. For a time he is a slave on a Turkish galley. The two robberies and the three plunderings by Arabs on land reported by Young Wilmot are Lillo's reversal and expansion of what was, in his sources, the son's piratical career.

OLD WILMOT. A rare example
Of Fortune's caprice, apter to surprise
Or entertain than comfort or instruct.
If you would reason from events, be just 90
And count, when you escaped, how many perished,
And draw your inference thence.

AGNES. Alas, who knows
But we were rend'red childless by some storm
In which you, though preserved, might bear a part?

YOUNG WILMOT (*aside*).
How has my curiosity betrayed me 95
Into superfluous pain! I faint with fondness,
And shall, if I stay longer, rush upon 'em,
Proclaim myself their son, kiss and embrace 'em
Till their souls, transported with the excess
Of pleasure and surprise, quit their frail mansions, 100
And leave 'em breathless in my longing arms.
By circumstances, then, and slow degrees
They must be let into a happiness
Too great for them to bear at once and live.
That Charlot shall perform. I need not feign 105
To ask an hour for rest. —Sir, I entreat
The favor to retire where, for a while,
I may repose myself. You will excuse
This freedom and the trouble that I give you.
'Tis long since I have slept, and Nature calls. 110

OLD WILMOT.
I pray, no more. Believe we're only troubled
That you should think any excuse were needful.

YOUNG WILMOT.
The weight of this is some encumbrance to me,

87. A rare example] *G, D1, D2–C;* A rare example of the caprice of Fortune *A. This must be a printer's error since l. 88 repeats the same idea.*
88. caprice] *G–H;* changes *C.*
93. rend'red] *G;* render'd *D1–H;* rendered *C.*
99–100.] *G, D2;* Until *A;* Till, with the excess of pleasure and surprise/ Their souls, transported, their frail mansions quit. *D1, H, C.*
109. that . . . you] *G, D1, D2–C;* which I give *A.*
113. is . . . me] *G, A, D2;* to me is some encumbrance *D1, H, C.*

Takes a casket out of his bosom, and gives it to his mother.

And its contents of value. If you please
To take the charge of it till I awake, 115
I shall not rest the worse. If I should sleep
Till I am asked for, as perhaps I may,
I beg that you would wake me.

AGNES. Doubt it not.
Distracted as I am with various woes,
I shall remember that. *Exit.*

YOUNG WILMOT. Merciless grief! 120
What ravage has it made! How has it changed
Her lovely form and mind! I feel her anguish,
And dread I know not what from her despair.
My father, too— Oh, grant 'em patience, Heaven,
A little longer, a few short hours more, 125
And all their cares and mine shall end forever.
How near is misery and joy allied!
Nor eye nor thought can their extremes divide.
A moment's space is long, and lightning slow,
To Fate descending to reverse our woe, 130
Or blast our hopes, and all our joys o'erthrow. *Exeunt.*

120. S.D.] *G–H;* (*Exit, with* Old Wilmot.) *C. Both of the elder Wilmots should leave the stage to allow for Young Wilmot's closing soliloquy. However, G, D1, D2, and C retain the final S.D.* (*Exeunt*), *which A and H omit.*

ACT III

[III.i] *The scene continued.*

Enter Agnes *alone, with the casket in her hand.*

[AGNES.]

Who should this stranger be? And then this casket—
He says it is of value, and yet trusts it,
As if a trifle, to a stranger's hand.
His confidence amazes me. Perhaps
It is not what he says. I'm strongly tempted 5
To open it and see. No, let it rest.
Why should my curiosity excite me
To search and pry into th'affairs of others,
Who have t'employ my thoughts so many cares
And sorrows of my own?—With how much ease 10
The spring gives way!—Surprising! most prodigious!
My eyes are dazzled and my ravished heart
Leaps at the glorious sight. How bright's the luster,
How immense the worth of these fair jewels!
Aye, such a treasure would expel forever 15
Base poverty and all its abject train:
The mean devices we're reduced to use
To keep out famine and preserve our lives
From day to day, the cold neglect of friends,
The galling scorn or more provoking pity 20
Of an insulting world. Possessed of these,
Plenty, content, and power might take their turn,
And lofty pride bare its aspiring head
At our approach and once more bend before us.
A pleasing dream!—'Tis past, and now I wake 25
More wretched by the happiness I've lost.

8. th'affairs] *G–H;* the cares *C.*
9–10. Who . . . own] *G–H;* Who have so many sorrows of my own *C.*
11. Most prodigious] *G–H; om. C.*
17–19. The . . . day] *G–H;* Famine *C.*
20. the galling scorn] *G–H;* the scorn *C.*
21. Of . . . world] *G–H;* of the world *C.*
21. Possessed of these] *G–H; om. C.*
26.] *G, A, D2; om. D1, H, C. Omission makes the following line obscure.*
26.] *A inserts a line* But wherefore lost?

For sure it was a happiness to think,
Though but a moment, such a treasure mine.
Nay, it was more than thought. I saw and touched
The bright temptation, and I see it yet. 30
'Tis here—'tis mine—I have it in possession!
Must I resign it? Must I give it back?
Am I in love with misery and want,
To rob myself and court so vast a loss?
Retain it, then! But how? There is a way— 35
Why sinks my heart? Why does my blood run cold?
Why am I thrilled with horror? 'Tis not choice,
But dire necessity, suggests the thought!

Enter Old Wilmot.

OLD WILMOT.
The mind contented, with how little pains
The wand'ring senses yield to soft repose 40
And die to gain new life! He's fallen asleep
Already. Happy man!—What dost thou think,
My Agnes, of our unexpected guest?
He seems to me a youth of great humanity.
Just ere he closed his eyes, that swam in tears, 45
He wrung my hand, and pressed it to his lips,
And, with a look that pierced me to the soul,
Begged me to comfort thee and—dost thou hear me?
What art thou gazing on? Fie, 'tis not well!
This casket was delivered to you closed. 50
Why have you opened it? Should this be known,
How mean must we appear!

AGNES.
And who shall know it?

OLD WILMOT.
There is a kind of pride, a decent dignity,
Due to ourselves, which, spite of our misfortunes,
May be maintained and cherished to the last. 55
To live without reproach, and without leave
To quit the world, shows sovereign contempt
And noble scorn of its relentless malice.

28. but a moment] *G–A, H, C;* but for a moment *D2.*
34. court] *G, D1, D2–C;* count *A.*
41. And . . . life] *G–H; om. C.*
43. our . . . guest] *G–H; om. C.*

AGNES.

Shows sovereign madness, and a scorn of sense!
Pursue no farther this detested theme. 60
I will not die, I will not leave the world,
For all that you can urge, until compelled.

OLD WILMOT.

To chase a shadow, when the setting sun
Is darting his last rays, were just as wise
As your anxiety for fleeting life, 65
Now the last means for its support are failing.
Were famine not as mortal as the sword,
This warmth might be excused. But take thy choice.
Die how you will, you shall not die alone.

AGNES.

Nor live, I hope.

OLD WILMOT. There is no fear of that. 70

AGNES.

Then we'll live both.

OLD WILMOT. Strange folly! Where's the means?

AGNES.

The means are there! Those jewels—

OLD WILMOT. Ha! Take heed!

Perhaps thou dost but try me; yet, take heed!
There's naught so monstrous but the mind of man
In some conditions may be brought t'approve. 75
Theft, sacrilege, treason, and parricide,
When flatt'ring opportunity enticed
And desperation drove, have been committed
By those who once would start to hear them named.

AGNES.

And add to these, detested suicide, 80
Which, by a crime much less, we may avoid.

65. As your anxiety] *G, D1, D2–C;* How vain th'anxiety *A.*
66. Now] *G, D1, D2–C;* When *A.*
68. This warmth] *G–H;* Your warmth *C.*
71. live both] *G, D1, D2–C;* both live *A. A also reverses Old Wilmot's exclamation and question.*
71. Where's] *G, D2;* Where *D1, H;* Where are *A, C.*
72. The . . . there!] *G, D2*; The means are here *A;* There! *D1, H, C.*
72. Those] *G, D1, D2–C;* These *A.*
77.] *G, D1, D2–C; om. A.*
78. And] *G, D1, D2–C;* When *A.*

OLD WILMOT.
Th'inhospitable murder of our guest!
How could'st thou form a thought so very tempting,
So advantageous, so secure, and easy,
And yet so cruel and so full of horror? 85

AGNES.
'Tis less impiety, less against nature,
To take another's life than end our own.

OLD WILMOT.
It is no matter whether this or that
Be, in itself, the less or greater crime.
Howe'er we may deceive ourselves or others, 90
We act from inclination, not by rule,
Or none could act amiss. And that all err,
None but the conscious hypocrite denies.
Oh, what is man, his excellence and strength,
When in an hour of trial and desertion, 95
Reason, his noblest power, may be suborned
To plead the cause of vile assassination?

AGNES.
You're too severe. Reason may justly plead
For her own preservation.

OLD WILMOT. Rest contented.
Whate'er resistance I may seem to make, 100
I am betrayed within. My will's seduced
And my whole soul infected. The desire
Of life returns, and brings with it a train
Of appetites that rage to be supplied.
Whoever stands to parley with temptation 105
Does it to be o'ercome.

82.] *A precedes with a line* What crime?
82.] *G–H; om. C.*
83. tempting] *G, D1, D2, H;* dreadful *A;* damning *C.*
84–85.] *A condenses to* So cruel, bloody, and so full of horror?
88–89.] *G–H;* No matter which, the greater or the lesser crime *C.*
90–97.] *G, D1, D2–C; see Appendix A for revision in A.*
99. her] *G–H;* our *C.*
99.] *A continues:* and these means/ Are given us to preserve our wretched beings./ His death alone gives us the means to live.
99–116.] *A revises and supplements these three speeches to make Old Wilmot's capitulation more comprehensible.*
106. Does it] *G, D1, D2, H;* Parlies *C.*

AGNES. Then naught remains
But the swift execution of a deed
That is not to be thought on or delayed.
We must dispatch him sleeping. Should he wake,
'Twere madness to attempt it.

OLD WILMOT. True, his strength 110
Single is more, much more than ours united.
So may his life, perhaps, as far exceed
Ours in duration, should he 'scape this snare.
Gen'rous, unhappy man! Oh, what could move thee
To put thy life and fortune in the hands 115
Of wretches mad with anguish?

AGNES. By what means,
By stabbing, suffocation, or by strangling,
Shall we effect his death?

OLD WILMOT. Why, what a fiend!
How cruel, how remorseless and impatient
Have pride and poverty made thee!

AGNES. Barbarous man! 120
Whose wasteful riots ruined our estate
And drove our son, ere the first down had spread
His rosy cheeks, spite of my sad presages,
Earnest entreaties, agonies, and tears,
To seek his bread 'mongst strangers, and to perish 125
In some remote, inhospitable land?
The loveliest youth, in person and in mind,
That ever crowned a groaning mother's pains!
Where was thy pity, where thy patience then?
Thou cruel husband! Thou unnat'ral father! 130
Thou most remorseless, most ungrateful man!
To waste my fortune, rob me of my son,
To drive me to despair, and then reproach me
For being what thou'st made me!

OLD WILMOT. Dry thy tears.

109–113.] *G, D1, D2, H; om. C.*
117.] *G–H; om. C.*
118. Why . . . fiend!] *G, D1, D2–C;* I cannot, will not do it! Oh, thou fiend! *A.*
122. had spread] *G, D1, D2–C;* o'erspread *A.*
122. down] *G–D2, C;* dawn *H.*
125. 'mongst] *G, D1, D2–C;* 'mong *A.*

I ought not to reproach thee. I confess 135
That thou hast suffered much. So have we both.
But chide no more; I'm wrought up to thy purpose.
The poor, ill-fated, unsuspecting victim,
Ere he reclined him on the fatal couch
From which he's ne'er to rise, took off the sash 140
And costly dagger that thou saw'st him wear,
And thus, unthinking, furnished us with arms
Against himself. Which shall I use?

AGNES. The sash.
If you make use of that, I can assist.

OLD WILMOT. No.
'Tis a dreadful office, and I'll spare 145
Thy trembling hands the guilt. Steal to the door
And bring me word if he be still asleep. *Exit* Agnes.
Or I'm deceived or he pronounced himself
The happiest of mankind. Deluded wretch!
Thy thoughts are perishing, thy youthful joys, 150
Touched by the icy hand of grisly Death,
Are with'ring in their bloom. —But, thought extinguished,
He'll never know the loss, nor feel the bitter
Pangs of disappointment. Then I was wrong
In counting him a wretch. To die well pleased 155
Is all the happiest of mankind can hope for.
To be a wretch is to survive the loss
Of every joy, and even hope itself,
As I have done. Why do I mourn him, then?
For, by the anguish of my tortured soul, 160
He's to be envied if compared with me.

Enter Agnes *with Young Wilmot's dagger.*

AGNES.
The stranger sleeps at present, but so restless

136.] *A inserts:* Thy sharp reproaches wring me to the soul./ Witness the bitter anguish of my heart./ Thy sufferings are more grievous than my own.
137.] *A inserts:* I'll do this deed of death, this deed of murder.
138. unsuspecting] *G, D1, D2–C; om. A.*
140. From . . . rise] *G, D1, D2–C; om. A.*
143–146. Which . . . guilt] *G–H; om. C.*
148. Or I'm] *G, D1, D2–C;* I'm *A.*
149. Deluded] *G, D1, D2–C;* Unhappy *A.*

His slumbers seem, they can't continue long.
Come, come, dispatch! Here, I've secured his dagger.

OLD WILMOT.
Oh, Agnes, Agnes! If there be a hell, 'tis just 165
We should expect it. *Goes to take the dagger but lets it fall.*

AGNES.
Nay, for shame! Shake off this panic, and be more yourself!

OLD WILMOT.
What's to be done? On what had we determined?

AGNES.
You're quite dismayed. I'll do
The deed myself. *Takes up the dagger.*

OLD WILMOT. Give me the fatal steel. 170
'Tis but a single murder
Necessity, impatience, and despair,
The three wide mouths of that true Cerberus,
Grim poverty, demands. They shall be stopped.
Ambition, persecution, and revenge 175
Devour their millions daily, and shall I—
But, follow me and see how little cause
You had to think there was the least remains
Of manhood, pity, mercy, or remorse
Left in this savage breast. *Going the wrong way.*

AGNES. Where do you go? 180
The street is that way!

OLD WILMOT. True! I had forgot.

AGNES.
Quite, quite confounded!

OLD WILMOT. Well, I recover.
I shall find the way. *Exit.*

AGNES. Oh, softly, softly!

164. Come . . . dispatch!] *G–H; om. C.*
167. Nay, for shame!] *G–H; om. C.*
168.] *A changes to:* How say ye? What's to be done?/ What would ye have me do?
169–170. I'll . . . myself] *G–H; om. C.*
166–171.] *These lines break the blank verse pattern and are variously arranged in the editions collated.*
174. demands] *G, A, D2;* demand *D1, H, C.*
178. remains] *G–H;* remain *C.*
182–183. Well . . . way] *G, D1, D2–C;* Well, I'm recovered./ This is the way. *A.*
183–199. Oh . . . Wilmot!] *See Appendix A for revisions in C.*

The least noise undoes us. —Still I fear him.
No, now he seems determined. —Oh, that pause, 185
That cowardly pause! His resolution fails.—
'Tis wisely done to lift your eyes to Heaven!
When did you pray before? I have no patience!—
How he surveys him! What a look was there!
How full of anguish, pity, and remorse! 190
He'll never do it. —Strike, or give it o'er!
No, he recovers. —But that trembling arm
May miss its aim and, if he fails, we're lost.
'Tis done! Oh, no! He lives; he struggles yet!

YOUNG WILMOT (*in another room*).
Oh, Father! Father!

AGNES. Quick! Repeat the blow! 195
What pow'r shall I invoke to aid thee, Wilmot?
Yet, hold thy hand!—Inconstant, wretched woman!
What, doth my heart recoil and bleed with him
Whose murder you contrived? Oh, Wilmot, Wilmot!
Exit Agnes.

Enter Charlot, *Maria*, Eustace, Randal, *and others.*

CHARLOT.
What strange neglect! The doors are all unbarred 200
And not a living creature to be seen.

Enter Old Wilmot *and* Agnes.

CHARLOT.
Sir, we are come to give and to receive
A thousand greetings. —Ha! What can this mean?
Why do you look with such amazement on us?
Are these your transports for your son's return? 205
Where is my Wilmot? Has he not been here?
Would he defer your happiness so long,
Or could a habit so disguise your son

195. Oh, Father! Father!] *G, D1, D2, H;* Oh, Heav'ns! Oh, mercy, mercy! *A.*
197. Yet, hold] *G, D1, D2, H;* Ha! no— Yet, hold *A.*
198.] *G, D1, D2, H;* My heart recoils, and now I bleed with him *A.*
199. you contrived] *G;* was contrived, *D2;* it contrived *D1, H;* I contrived *A.*
199.1.] *C om.* Maria, *and others.*

That you refused to own him?

AGNES. Heard you that?

What prodigy of horror is disclosing 210

To render murder venial!

OLD WILMOT. Prithee, peace!

The miserable damned suspend their howling,

And the swift orbs are fixed in deep attention.

YOUNG WILMOT (*groans*).

Oh! Oh! Oh!

EUSTACE.

Sure, that deep groan came from the inner room. 215

RANDAL.

It did, and seemed the voice of one expiring.

Merciful Heaven! Where will these terrors end?

That is the dagger my young master wore,

And, see, his father's hands are stained with blood!

Young Wilmot *groans again.*

EUSTACE.

Another groan! Why do we stand to gaze 220

On these dumb phantoms of despair and horror?

Let us search farther. Randal, show the way.

CHARLOT.

This is the third time those fantastic forms

Have forced themselves upon my mental eyes

And, sleeping, gave me, more than waking, pains. 225

O you Eternal Powers! If all Your mercy

To wretched mortals be not quite extinguished

And terrors only guard Your awful thrones,

Remove this dreadful vision. Let me wake,

Or sleep the sleep of death.

Exeunt Charlot, *Maria*, Eustace, Randal, *&c.*

211–213. Prithee ... attention] *G, D1, D2–C; om. A.*

214–220. Oh! ... way] *G–H; see Appendix A for substitution in C.*

223–231.] *G–H; om. C.*

210–211. *disclosing ... venial*] disclosing itself to make ordinary murder (as contrasted with this murder of a son) venial.

213. *swift ... fixed*] This may mean that the planets have become fixed stars, or that the tortured and roving eyes of the damned are now fixed upon the Wilmots.

OLD WILMOT. Sleep those who may. 230
I know my lot is endless perturbation.

AGNES.
Let life forsake the earth, and light the sun,
And death and darkness bury in oblivion
Mankind and all their deeds, that no posterity
May ever rise to hear our horrid tale 235
Or view the graves of such detested parricides.

OLD WILMOT.
Curses and deprecations are in vain.
The sun will shine, and all things have their course,
When we, the curse and burden of the earth,
Shall be absorbed and mingled with its dust. 240
Our guilt and desolation must be told
From age to age to teach desponding mortals
How far beyond the reach of human thought
Heaven, when incensed, can punish. —Die thou first.
Stabs Agnes.
I dare not trust thy weakness.

AGNES. Ever kind, 245
But most in this!

OLD WILMOT. I will not long survive thee.

AGNES.
Do not accuse thy erring mother, Wilmot,
With too much rigor when we meet above.
Rivers of tears and ages spent in howling
Could ne'er express the anguish of my heart. 250
To give thee life for life, and blood for blood,
Is not enough. Had I ten thousand lives
I'd give them all to speak my penitence,
Deep, and sincere, and equal to my crime. *Dies.*

Enter Charlot, *led by Maria and* Randal; Eustace *and the rest.*

237. deprecations] *G–A, H, C;* depredations *D2.*
244–245. Die . . . weakness] *G, D1, D2–C;* Take this./ I need not bid thee use it now. (*Gives a dagger.*)/ Death now has lost its terror. *A.*
245. dare] *G, D1, D2, H;* durst *C.*
246.] *In A, Agnes* (*Lady Wilmot*) *stabs herself.*
249–250.] *G–H; om. C.*
254.1.] *G, D1, D2, H;* Charlot *led into the room by her maid. A;* (*Enter* Randal, Eustace.) *C.*

CHARLOT.

Welcome, Despair! I'll never hope again. 255
Why have you forced me from my Wilmot's side?
Let me return! Unhand me! Let me die!
Patience, that till this moment ne'er forsook me,
Has took her flight, and my abandoned mind,
Rebellious to a lot so void of mercy 260
And so unexpected, rages to madness.
O Thou, Who know'st our frame, Who know'st these woes
Are more than human fortitude can bear,
Oh, take me, take me hence, ere I relapse
And in distraction, with unhallowed tongue, 265
Again arraign Your mercy! *Faints.*

EUSTACE.

Unhappy maid! This strange event my strength
Can scarce support; no wonder thine should fail.
How shall I vent my grief? Oh, Wilmot, Wilmot!
Thou truest lover, and thou best of friends 270
Are these the fruits of all thy anxious cares
For thy ungrateful parents? Cruel fiends!
To use thee thus, to recompense with death
Thy most unequalled duty and affection!

OLD WILMOT.

What whining fool art thou who would'st usurp 275
My sovereign right of grief? Was he thy son?
Say! Canst thou show thy hands reeking with blood
That flowed, through purer channels, from thy loins?

EUSTACE.

Forbid it, Heaven, that I should know such guilt!
Yet his sad fate demands commiseration. 280

OLD WILMOT.

Compute the sands that bound the spacious ocean
And swell their number with a single grain;
Increase the noise of thunder with thy voice;
Or, when the raging wind lays nature waste,
Assist the tempest with thy feeble breath; 285

255–269. Welcome . . . grief?] *G–H; om. C.*
270.] *G–H; om. C.*
273–274.] *G–H; om. C.*
279–280.] *G–H; om. C.*

Add water to the sea, and fire to Etna—
But name not thy faint sorrow with the anguish
Of a cursed wretch who only hopes for this *Stabbing himself.*
To change the scene, but not relieve his pain!

RANDAL.
A dreadful instance of the last remorse! 290
May all your woes end here.

OLD WILMOT. Oh, would they end
A thousand ages hence, I then should suffer
Much less than I deserve. Yet let me say
You'll do but justice to inform the world
This horrid deed that punishes itself 295
Was not intended as he was our son;
For that we knew not, till it was too late.
Proud and impatient under our afflictions,
While Heaven was laboring to make us happy,
We brought this dreadful ruin on ourselves. 300
Mankind may learn—but—oh! *Dies.*

RANDAL. The most will not.
Let us at least be wiser, nor complain
Of Heaven's mysterious ways and awful reign.
By our bold censures we invade His throne
Who made mankind and governs but His own. 305
Though youthful Wilmot's sun be set ere noon,
The ripe in virtue never die too soon. *Exeunt.*

FINIS

288. for] *G, A, D2;* from *D1, H, C.*
296. as he was] *G–H;* thinking him *C.*
301. The . . . not] *G, D1, D2, H;* Heaven grant they may! *C; om. A. See Appendix A.*
302–307.] *G–H; see Appendix A for lines substituted in C.*

Appendix A

Variant and Additional Passages

[II.iii.36]
A inserts before Sir: Old Wilmot *opens the letter, which was as follows:* Sir, The unhappy bearer of this letter is one of those Gentlemen that was so unfortunately ship-wreck'd last night off Falmouth; and, as he is my valu'd ſriend, (though an object of distress) pray be kind enough to receive him under your protection, 'till such time I can embrace the opportunity of paying my best respects to you in person, which I propose doing this evening. Your's, &c. With all due esteem. Charlot Borlaise. Penryn, Cornwall.

[III.i.90–97]
A revises to:

They both are crimes; let neither be committed.
What art thou, Agnes,
When in an hour of trial and suffrance,
Reason, thy noblest power, is thus suborned
To plead the cause of murder?

[III.i.183–199]
C omits Young Wilmot's cry (l. 195) and combines, condenses, and alters the tone of Agnes's speeches:

Oh, softly! softly! The least noise undoes us!
What are we doing? Misery and want
Are lighter ills than this! I cannot bear it!
Stop! Hold thy hand! —Inconstant, wretched woman!
What! Doth my heart recoil? Oh, Wilmot, Wilmot!
What pow'r shall I invoke to aid thee, Wilmot?

[III.i.214–222]
C substitutes:

RANDAL.
What mean these dreadful words and frantic air?

EUSTACE.

My mind misgives me. Do not stand to gaze
On these dumb phantoms of despair and horror!
Let us search further. Randal, show the way. (*Exeunt.*)
(*Manent* Old Wilmot *and* Agnes.)

[III.i.301]
A inserts: Charlot *returns with* Maria, *in a great rage, tearing her hair, &c. with agonies of death strongly on her.*

CHARLOT.

Oh where is my dear Wilmot?
Why do you keep him from me?
Hark! I hear him groan!
He calls me to him to take an everlasting farewell.

MARIA.

Be patient, dear madam.

CHARLOT.

Talkst thou to me of patience?
No, I am wretched
And will not live without my Wilmot.
What's here? A dagger?
Ah, that fatal dagger
That robbed me of my love,
And thus it ends a miserable life. (*Stabs herself.*)

[III.i.302–307]
C substitutes:

And may thy penitence atone thy crime!
'Tend well the hapless Charlot, and bear hence
These bleeding victims of despair and pride.
Toll the death bell, and follow to the grave
The wretched parents and ill-fated son.

Appendix B

The Source of *Fatal Curiosity*

The original source of the plot of *Fatal Curiosity* was probably a black-letter pamphlet entitled *Newes from Perin in Cornwall Of A most Bloody and un-exampled Murther very lately committed by a Father on his owne Sonne (who was lately returned from the Indyes) at the Instigation of a mercilesse Step-mother* . . . (London: Printed by E. A., 1618). This pamphlet was condensed by Sir William Sanderson and included in his *Compleat History of the Lives and Reigns of Mary Queen of Scotland, And of Her Son and Successor, James the Sixth, King of Scotland* . . . (London: Printed for Humphrey Moseley, Richard Tomlins, and George Sawbridge, 1656).[1] In turn, Sanderson's account was repeated almost verbatim in *The Annals of King James and King Charles the First* (London: Printed by Thomas Bradyll, for Robert Clavel, 1681), which, though published anonymously, was known as *Frankland's Annals*.[2]

Lillo could have read all three of these publications, but it is almost certain that he based his play upon the accounts in the histories rather than upon the pamphlet. The main reason for this conclusion is the fact that both Sanderson and Frankland discuss the fall of Sir

[1] Sanderson omitted many details of the son's piratical adventures and Turkish enslavement, as well as an elaborate description of the final shipwreck. He curtailed a stylized passage dealing with the triple temptation of the husband by the wife and omitted supernatural elements such as a drop of blood falling from the murderer's nose upon the victim's breast and the warning cry of an owl. He also changed the sister from an innkeeper's wife to a mercer's wife, the identifying mole to a scar on the son's arm, and the stepmother to the actual mother.

[2] *Frankland's Annals* has several typographical errors, such as "Perinin," "kitching fire," and "could season," but the only important variation from Sanderson is the substitution of "Majesty" for "Misery" (l. 26). This would seem to mean that the King personally sponsored the returned captive. However, both words may be misprints for "Master" in the original pamphlet. The passage in *Newes from Perin* reads: "His Master sent him Surgeon in a Ship to the Indies."

Walter Ralegh in 1618 and conclude that, although he was a worthy gentleman, he lacked "inward grace." They then piously urge the reader to pray for Divine protection against temptation and, as an exemplum of "the miserable condition of sinful man," they next report the story of the "monstrous murther in Cornwal." That Lillo should open his play with a lengthy discussion of Ralegh's imprisonment (I.i.29–50) and then proceed to the tragedy of the Wilmots can hardly be coincidental.[3] One may also note that Lillo follows the annalists in changing the wicked stepmother of the pamphlet to the victim's real mother.

The text of this appendix, which I have modernized, is taken from the first edition of *A Compleat History of the Lives and Reigns of Mary Queen of Scotland, And of Her Son and Successor, James the Sixth, King of Scotland . . . By William Sanderson, Esq.* (London, 1656), pp. 463–465.

ANNO 1618. A MONSTROUS MURDER IN CORNWALL.

The miserable condition of sinful man in sundry examples of these present and of former times should mind us hourly to beg of God preventing grace, lest we fall into temptations of sin and Satan. Such have been the calamities of ages past, at present are, and will be to come: stories of theft, 5
rapine, murders, and such like.

One of wondrous note happened at Perin in Cornwall in September, a bloody and unexampled murder by a father and mother upon their only son, and then upon themselves.

He had been blessed with ample possessions and fruitful 10
issue, unhappy only in a younger son, who, taking liberty from his father's bounty, and with a crew of like condition that wearied on land, they went roving to sea, and, in a small vessel southward, took boot from all whom they could master, and so, increasing force and wealth, ventured 15
on a Turk's man in the Straits but, by mischance, their own powder fired themselves. And our gallant, trusting to his skilful swimming, got shore upon Rhodes with the best of his jewels about him, where, offering some to sale to a

[3] *Newes from Perin . . .* does not mention Ralegh.

16. *Turk's man*] Turkish man-of-war.

Jew, who knew them to be the Governor's of Algiers, he was 20
apprehended and, as a pirate, sentenced to the galleys
among other Christians, whose miserable slavery made
them all studious of freedom, and with wit and valor took
opportunity and means to murder some officers, got aboard
of an English ship, and came safe to London; where his 25
misery and some skill made him servant to a surgeon, and
sudden preferment to the East Indies. There, by this means,
he got money, with which returning back, he designed himself for his native county, Cornwall. And in a small ship
from London, sailing to the west, was cast away upon that 30
coast. But his excellent skill in swimming, and former fate
to boot, brought him safe to shore, where, since his fifteen
years' absence, his father's former fortunes much decayed,
now retired him not far off to a country habitation in debt
and danger. 35

His sister he finds married to a mercer, a meaner match
than her birth promised. To her at first he appears a poor
stranger, but in private reveals himself, and withal what
jewels and gold he had concealed in a bow-case about him.
And concluded that the next day he intended to appear to 40
his parents, and to keep his disguise till she and her husband
should meet and make their common joy complete.

Being come to his parents, his humble behavior, suitable
to his suit of clothes, melted the old couple to so much compassion as to give him covering from the cold season under 45
their outward roof, and by degrees his traveling tales told
with passion to the aged people made him their guest so long
by the kitchen fire that the husband took leave and went to
bed. And soon after, his true stories working compassion in
the weaker vessel, she wept and so did he. But, compas- 50
sionate of her tears, he comforted her with a piece of gold,
which gave assurance that he deserved a lodging, to which
she brought him. And, being in bed, showed her his girdled
wealth, which he said was sufficient to relieve her husband's

---

32–33. *fifteenth . . . absence*] Lillo reduces this absence to the more traditional seven years (I.iii.69) of the Bible and folklore. See also Maria's song (I.ii.24).

39. *bow-case*] a curved container worn around the waist. The account later mentions his "girdled wealth."

wants and to spare for himself, and, being very weary, fell fast asleep. 55

The wife, tempted with the golden bait of what she had and eager of enjoying all, awaked her husband with this news and her contrivance what to do. And, though with horrid apprehension he oft refused, yet her puling fondness (Eve's enchantment) moved him to consent and rise to be master of all, and both of them to murder the man, which they instantly did, covering the corpse under the clothes till opportunity to convey it out of the way. 60

The early morning hastens the sister to her father's house where she, with signs of joy, inquires for a sailor that should lodge there the last night. The parents slightly denied to have seen any such until she told them that he was her brother, her lost brother; by that assured scar upon his arm cut with a sword in his youth she knew him; and were all resolved this morning to meet there and be merry. 65 70

The father hastily runs up, finds the mark, and, with horrid regret at this monstrous murder of his own son, with the same knife cut his own throat.

The wife went up to consult with him, where, in a most strange manner beholding them both in blood, wild and aghast, with the instrument at hand, readily rips up her own belly till the guts tumbled out. 75

The daughter, doubting the delays of their absence, searches for them all, whom she found out too soon. With the sad sight of this scene, and being overcome with horror and amaze of this deluge of destruction, she sank down and died—the fatal end of that family. 80

The truth of which was frequently known, and flew to Court in this guise, but the imprinted relation conceals their names in favor to some neighbor of repute and kin to that family. 85

The same sense makes me therein silent also.

---

60. *puling*] whining.

Appendix C

Chronology

Approximate years are indicated by *

Political and Literary Events	*Life and Major Works of Lillo*
1631 Death of Donne. John Dryden born.	
1633 Samuel Pepys born.	
1635 Sir George Etherege born.*	
1640 Aphra Behn born.*	
1641 William Wycherley born.*	
1642 First Civil War began (ended 1646). Theaters closed by Parliament. Thomas Shadwell born.*	
1648 Second Civil War.	
1649 Execution of Charles I.	
1650 Jeremy Collier born.	
1651 Hobbes' *Leviathan* published.	
1652 First Dutch War began (ended 1654). Thomas Otway born.	

1653

Nathaniel Lee born.*

1656

D'Avenant's *THE SIEGE OF RHODES* performed at Rutland House.

1657

John Dennis born.

1658

Death of Cromwell.

D'Avenant's *THE CRUELTY OF THE SPANIARDS IN PERU* performed at the Cockpit.

1660

Restoration of Charles II.

Theatrical patents granted to Thomas Killigrew and Sir William D'Avenant, authorizing them to form, respectively, the King's and the Duke of York's Companies.

Pepys began his diary.

1661

Cowley's *THE CUTTER OF COLEMAN STREET.*

D'Avenant's *THE SIEGE OF RHODES* (expanded to two parts).

1662

Charter granted to the Royal Society.

1663

Dryden's *THE WILD GALLANT.*

Tuke's *THE ADVENTURES OF FIVE HOURS.*

1664

Sir John Vanbrugh born.

Dryden's *THE RIVAL LADIES.*

Dryden and Howard's *THE INDIAN QUEEN.*

Etherege's *THE COMICAL REVENGE.*

1665

Second Dutch War began (ended 1667).

Great Plague.

Dryden's *THE INDIAN EMPEROR.*
Orrery's *MUSTAPHA.*

1666
Fire of London.
Death of Shirley.

1667
Jonathan Swift born.
Milton's *Paradise Lost* published.
Sprat's *The History of the Royal Society* published.
Dryden's *SECRET LOVE.*

1668
Death of D'Avenant.
Dryden made Poet Laureate.
Dryden's *An Essay of Dramatic Poesy* published.
Shadwell's *THE SULLEN LOVERS.*

1669
Pepys terminated his diary.
Susannah Centlivre born.

1670
William Congreve born.
Dryden's *THE CONQUEST OF GRANADA*, Part I.

1671
Dorset Garden Theatre (Duke's Company) opened.
Colley Cibber born.
Milton's *Paradise Regained* and *Samson Agonistes* published.
Dryden's *THE CONQUEST OF GRANADA*, Part II.
THE REHEARSAL, by the Duke of Buckingham and others.
Wycherley's *LOVE IN A WOOD.*

1672
Third Dutch War began (ended 1674).
Joseph Addison born.
Richard Steele born.
Dryden's *MARRIAGE À LA MODE.*

1674

New Drury Lane Theatre (King's Company) opened.

Death of Milton.

Nicholas Rowe born.

Thomas Rymer's *Reflections on Aristotle's Treatise of Poesy* (translation of Rapin) published.

1675

Dryden's *AURENG-ZEBE.*

Wycherley's *THE COUNTRY WIFE.**

1676

Etherege's *THE MAN OF MODE.*

Otway's *DON CARLOS.*

Shadwell's *THE VIRTUOSO.*

Wycherley's *THE PLAIN DEALER.*

1677

Rymer's *Tragedies of the Last Age Considered* published.

Aphra Behn's *THE ROVER.*

Dryden's *ALL FOR LOVE.*

Lee's *THE RIVAL QUEENS.*

1678

Popish Plot.

George Farquhar born.

Bunyan's *Pilgrim's Progress* (Part I) published.

1679

Exclusion Bill introduced.

Death of Thomas Hobbes.

Death of Roger Boyle, Earl of Orrery.

Charles Johnson born.

1680

Death of Samuel Butler.

Death of John Wilmot, Earl of Rochester.

Dryden's *THE SPANISH FRIAR.*

Lee's *LUCIUS JUNIUS BRUTUS.*

Otway's *THE ORPHAN.*

Chronology

1681

Charles II dissolved Parliament at Oxford.

Dryden's *Absalom and Achitophel* published.

Tate's adaptation of *KING LEAR*.

1682

The King's and the Duke of York's Companies merged into the United Company.

Dryden's *The Medal*, *MacFlecknoe*, and *Religio Laici* published.

Otway's *VENICE PRESERVED*.

1683

Rye House Plot.

Death of Thomas Killigrew.

Crowne's *CITY POLITIQUES*.

1685

Death of Charles II; accession of James II.

Revocation of the Edict of Nantes.

The Duke of Monmouth's Rebellion.

Death of Otway.

John Gay born.

Crowne's *SIR COURTLY NICE*.

Dryden's *ALBION AND ALBANIUS*.

1687

Death of the Duke of Buckingham.

Dryden's *The Hind and the Panther* published.

Newton's *Principia* published.

1688

The Revolution.

Alexander Pope born.

Shadwell's *THE SQUIRE OF ALSATIA*.

1689

The War of the League of Augsburg began (ended 1697).

Toleration Act.

Death of Aphra Behn.
Shadwell made Poet Laureate.
Dryden's *DON SEBASTIAN*.
Shadwell's *BURY FAIR*.

1690
Battle of the Boyne.
Locke's *Two Treatises of Government* and *An Essay Concerning Human Understanding* published.

1691
Death of Etherege.
Langbaine's *An Account of the English Dramatic Poets* published.

1692
Death of Lee.
Death of Shadwell.
Tate made Poet Laureate.

1693
Rymer's *A Short View of Tragedy* published.
Congreve's *THE OLD BACHELOR*.

George Lillo born in London.*

1694
Death of Queen Mary.
Southerne's *THE FATAL MARRIAGE*.

1695
Group of actors led by Thomas Betterton left Drury Lane and established a new company at Lincoln's Inn Fields.
Congreve's *LOVE FOR LOVE*.
Southerne's *OROONOKO*.

1696
Cibber's *LOVE'S LAST SHIFT*.
Vanbrugh's *THE RELAPSE*.

1697
Treaty of Ryswick ended the War of the League of Augsburg.
Charles Macklin born.
Congreve's *THE MOURNING BRIDE*.
Vanbrugh's *THE PROVOKED WIFE*.

1698

Collier controversy started with the publication of *A Short View of the Immorality and Profaneness of the English Stage*.

1699

Farquhar's *THE CONSTANT COUPLE*.

1700

Death of Dryden.

Blackmore's *Satire against Wit* published.

Congreve's *THE WAY OF THE WORLD*.

1701

Act of Settlement.

War of the Spanish Succession began (ended 1713).

Death of James II.

Rowe's *TAMERLANE*.

Steele's *THE FUNERAL*.

1702

Death of William III; accession of Anne.

The Daily Courant began publication.

Cibber's *SHE WOULD AND SHE WOULD NOT*.

1703

Death of Pepys.

Rowe's *THE FAIR PENITENT*.

1704

Capture of Gibraltar; Battle of Blenheim.

Defoe's *The Review* began publication (1704–1713).

Swift's *A Tale of a Tub* and *The Battle of the Books* published.

Cibber's *THE CARELESS HUSBAND*.

1705

Haymarket Theatre opened.

Steele's *THE TENDER HUSBAND*.

1706
Battle of Ramillies.
Farquhar's *THE RECRUITING OFFICER.*
1707
Union of Scotland and England.
Death of Farquhar.
Henry Fielding born.
Farquhar's *THE BEAUX' STRATAGEM.*
1708
Downes' *Roscius Anglicanus* published.
1709
Samuel Johnson born.
Rowe's edition of Shakespeare published.
The Tatler began publication (1709–1711).
Centlivre's *THE BUSY BODY.*
1711
Shaftesbury's *Characteristics* published.
The Spectator began publication (1711–1712).
Pope's *An Essay on Criticism* published.
1713
Treaty of Utrecht ended the War of the Spanish Succession.
Addison's *CATO.*
1714
Death of Anne; accession of George I.
Steele became Governor of Drury Lane.
John Rich assumed management of Lincoln's Inn Fields.
Centlivre's *THE WONDER: A WOMAN KEEPS A SECRET.*
Rowe's *JANE SHORE.*
1715
Jacobite Rebellion.

Death of Tate.
Rowe made Poet Laureate.
Death of Wycherley.
1716
Addison's *THE DRUMMER.*
1717
David Garrick born.
Cibber's *THE NON-JUROR.*
Gay, Pope, and Arbuthnot's *THREE HOURS AFTER MARRIAGE.*
1718
Death of Rowe.
Centlivre's *A BOLD STROKE FOR A WIFE.*
1719
Death of Addison.
Defoe's *Robinson Crusoe* published.
Young's *BUSIRIS, KING OF EGYPT.*
1720
South Sea Bubble.
Samuel Foote born.
Steele suspended from the Governorship of Drury Lane (restored 1721).
Little Theatre in the Haymarket opened.
Steele's *The Theatre* (periodical) published.
Hughes' *THE SIEGE OF DAMASCUS.*
1721
Walpole became first Minister.
1722
Steele's *THE CONSCIOUS LOVERS.*
1723
Death of Susannah Centlivre.
Death of D'Urfey.
1725
Pope's edition of Shakespeare published.

1726
Death of Jeremy Collier.
Death of Vanbrugh.
Law's *Unlawfulness of Stage Entertainments* published.
Swift's *Gulliver's Travels* published.

1727
Death of George I; accession of George II.
Death of Sir Isaac Newton.
Arthur Murphy born.

1728
Pope's *The Dunciad* (first version) published.
Cibber's *THE PROVOKED HUSBAND* (expansion of Vanbrugh's fragment *A JOURNEY TO LONDON*).
Gay's *THE BEGGAR'S OPERA.*

1729
Goodman's Fields Theatre opened.
Death of Congreve.
Death of Steele.
Edmund Burke born.

1730
Cibber made Poet Laureate.
Oliver Goldsmith born.
Thomson's *The Seasons* published.
Fielding's *THE AUTHOR'S FARCE.*
Fielding's *TOM THUMB* (revised as *THE TRAGEDY OF TRAGEDIES*, 1731).

SYLVIA; OR, THE COUNTRY BURIAL.

1731
Death of Defoe.
Fielding's *THE GRUB-STREET OPERA.*

THE LONDON MERCHANT; OR, THE HISTORY OF GEORGE BARNWELL.

1732
Covent Garden Theatre opened.
Death of Gay.
George Colman the elder born.
Fielding's *THE COVENT GARDEN TRAGEDY.*

Fielding's *THE MODERN HUSBAND.*

Charles Johnson's *CAELIA.*

1733

Pope's *An Essay on Man* (Epistles I–III) published (Epistle IV, 1734).

1734

Death of Dennis.

THE CHRISTIAN HERO.

The Prompter began publication (1734–1736).

Theobald's edition of Shakespeare published.

Fielding's *DON QUIXOTE IN ENGLAND.*

1736

Fielding led the "Great Mogul's Company of Comedians" at the Little Theatre in the Haymarket (1736–1737).

GUILT ITS OWN PUNISHMENT; OR, FATAL CURIOSITY.

Fielding's *PASQUIN.*

1737

The Stage Licensing Act.

Dodsley's *THE KING AND THE MILLER OF MANSFIELD.*

Fielding's *THE HISTORICAL REGISTER FOR 1736.*

1738

Johnson's *London* published.

Pope's *One Thousand Seven Hundred and Thirty-Eight* published.

MARINA.

Swift's *A Complete Collection of Genteel and Ingenious Conversation* published.

Thomson's *AGAMEMNON.*

1739

War with Spain began.

Death of George Lillo.

Hugh Kelly born.

Fielding's *The Champion* began publication (1739–1741).

Johnson's *Complete Vindication of Licensers of the Stage*, an ironical criticism of the Licensing Act, published after Brooke's *GUSTAVUS VASA* was denied a license.